IELTS Speaking

Guide to achieve band 8 or more

by

Sampath Bandara

ISBN: 1537436082
ISBN-13: 978-1537436081

Dedication

I dedicate this study guide to the students who are trying to get a good band score in IELTS. I can assure that this study guide will surely help you to achieve a good score. Try to practice well and be prepared before you take the IELTS speaking test. Always follow the instructions given here so as to get good results.

Contents

Acknowledgements

I take this opportunity to acknowledge everyone who helped me in every other way to bring this book to be published. Thank you everyone who encourage me in many ways to write this study guide.

My special thanks go to my beloved wife Sandamini Heshani Alahakoon, who was with me every time and will be with me forever. Unless her, this guide may not be written and published. Thank you for being with me and encouraging me to write this book.

I specially thank to my loving parents and my dear loving brothers who were with me always and gave their support and valuable ideas every time.

Sampath Bandara

IELTS Introduction

The International English Language Testing System (ILETS) measures the proficiency of the language of people who want to study or work in countries where used English as the main language of communication. The proficiency level is identified using a scale of 9-band. In this scale band score 1 is used for non-user and band score 9 is used for expert.

IELTS is available in two test formats. They are Academic and General Training. This provides a valid and accurate measurement of the four language skills: listening, reading, writing and speaking.

IELTS Academic

For the people applying for higher education or professional registration in an English speaking country must do IELTS Academic test.

IELTS General Training

Those who are going to English speaking countries for secondary education, work or training programs must do the IELTS General Training. To migrate to countries like Australia, Canada, New Zealand and the UK, this is a requirement too.

Test format

Listening and Speaking is same for both test types and Reading and Writing will be different according to the test type.

For Academic test:

Listening
Academic Reading
Academic Writing
Speaking

For General Training:

Listening

General Training Reading

General Training Writing

Speaking

The total test time is 2 hours and 45 minutes. Listening, Reading and Writing components should be completed on the same day with no breaks in between them. The Speaking test will be either after a break on the same day or up to a week before or after the other tests. This depends on the test center.

IELTS scale

Band score	Skill level	Description
9	Expert User	The test taker has fully operational command of the language. Their use of English is appropriate, accurate and fluent, and shows complete understanding.
8	Very good user	The test taker has fully operational command of the language with only occasional unsystematic inaccuracies and inappropriate usage. They may misunderstand some things in unfamiliar situations. They handle complex and detailed argumentation well.
7	Good user	The test taker has operational command of the language, though with occasional inaccuracies, inappropriate usage and misunderstandings in some situations. They generally handle complex language well and understand detailed reasoning.
6	Competent user	The test taker has an effective command of the language despite some inaccuracies, inappropriate usage and misunderstandings. They can use and understand fairly complex language, particularly in familiar situations.

5	Modest user	The test taker has a partial command of the language and copes with overall meaning in most situations, although they are likely to make many mistakes. They should be able to handle basic communication in their own field.
4	Limited user	The test taker's basic competence is limited to familiar situations. They frequently show problems in understanding and expression. They are not able to use complex language.
3	Extremely limited user	The test taker conveys and understands only general meaning in very familiar situations. There are frequent breakdowns in communication.
2	Intermittent user	The test taker has great difficulty understanding spoken and written English.
1	Non-user	The test taker has no ability to use the language except a few isolated words.
0	Did not attempt the test	The test taker did not answer the questions.

Overall band score

For each test component, Listening, Reading, Writing and Speaking, a score is given. These individual test scores are then averaged and rounded to produce an overall band score.

Marking and assessment of the Speaking test

The performances of speaking are assessed by the certified IELTS examiners. All the examiners hold teaching qualifications and are recruited as examiners by the test centers and approved by British Council or IDP: IELTS Australia. Scores are reported in whole and half bands according to the following criteria.

Fluency and coherence:

This criterion refers to the ability to talk with normal levels of continuity, rate and effort and to link ideas and language together to form coherent, connected speech. The key indicators of fluency are speech rate and speech continuity. The key indicators of coherence are logical sequencing of sentences, clear marking of stages in a discussion, narration or argument, and the use of cohesive devices (e.g. connectors, pronouns and conjunctions) within and between sentences.

Lexical resource:

This criterion refers to the range of vocabulary the test takers can use and the precision with which meanings and attitudes can be expressed. The key indicators are the variety of words used the adequacy and appropriate of the words used and the ability to circumlocution (get round a vocabulary gap by using other words) with or without noticeable hesitation.

Grammatical range and accuracy:

This criterion refers to the range and the accurate and appropriate use of the test takers' grammatical resource. The key indicators of grammatical range are the length and complexity of the spoken sentences, the appropriate use of subordinate clauses, and the range of sentence structures, especially to move elements around for information focus. The key indicators of grammatical accuracy are the number of grammatical errors in a given amount of speech and the communicative effect of error.

Pronunciation:

This criterion refers to the ability to produce comprehensible speech to fulfill the Speaking test requirements. The key indicators will be the amount of strain caused to the listener, the amount of the speech which is unintelligible and the noticeability of L1 influence.

Speaking test format

In this IELTS book, we are talking about the Speaking component only. The reason is, it is more important to get a high band score for the Speaking component. If you are going to work or do your higher studies in a country which uses English as the main communication language, you must have a high band score for the Speaking component. Otherwise you will not understand what others are saying and you will not communicate with the people efficiently. And the other important thing is most of the students are afraid of this test because they can't speak English fluently. Most of the Universities require more than 6 or 6.5 band score for the Speaking component.

This component measures your use of spoken English. The test takes between 11 and 14 minutes to complete. And importantly remember that every test is recorded by the examiner. This test consists of three parts.

Speaking Part 1

In this part the examiner is asking general questions about yourself and some familiar topics such as family, work, studies, friends, hobbies, sports, etc. This part lasts between 4 and 5 minutes.

Things you should do:

➢ You should have a good confident. And especially you should be friendly. Eye-contact is a must.
➢ There should be an excitement while you speak.
➢ You should have a good vocabulary. For example you can use cuisine for food.
➢ Rather than saying I like, you should use another phrases like I enjoy, I really love, I prefer.
➢ You should expand your answers. For example you can give examples.
➢ Always remember that practice is the key. Keep practicing until you feel confident while speaking. Keep practicing until words come to your mouth like water flows.

Things you shouldn't do:

- ➢ Don't speak with a monotone. Vary your voice accordingly.
- ➢ Don't just give yes/no answers. Expand your answer appropriately.
- ➢ Always remember not to repeat the question.
- ➢ Don't go off topic while you are speaking.
- ➢ Don't answer I don't know. Be smart when you have to speak what you don't know.
- ➢ Don't speak too quickly or slowly.
- ➢ Don't speak quietly as well.
- ➢ Always remember not to worry about perfect English.

Always remember that to get a good band score for this section you have to practice well. You should have a fluent speaking ability. It isn't come naturally if you are not a native speaker. For that you have to practice more. We can use some dialogs to practice daily speaking topics and have a good vocabulary. Here I give you 50 dialogs to practice well. Remember to practice these dialogs as much as possible. Speak loudly like you did as a child. Don't be shy to speak loudly. Speaking is a habit. We can have any habit doing it. To become a habit, we have to do it so many times. Think about this. If you want to swim, you have to go to a pool and start to practice it. If you are reading a book to learn how to swim, will you able to swim? Your reading ability will increase and you will have a good knowledge of swimming. But you won't swim. If you start to practice swimming rather than reading a book to learn swimming, you will become a good swimmer. English is also like that. Speaking is a habit. We must keep practicing speaking so as to become fluent in speaking. So practice these dialogs as much as possible.

Dialog 1 : Meeting someone new.

Jack : Hello.

Linda : Hi.

Jack : How are you?

Linda : I'm good. How are you?

Jack : Good. Do you speak English?

Linda : A little. Are you American?

Jack : Yes.

Linda : Where are you from?

Jack : I'm from California.

Linda : Nice to meet you.

Jack : Nice to meet you too.

Dialog 2 : Do you speak English?

Linda : Excuse me, are you American?

Jack : No.

Linda : Do you speak English?

Jack : A little, but not very well.

Linda : How long have you been here?

Jack : 2months.

Linda : What do you do for work?

Jack	: I'm a student. How about you?
Linda	: I'm a student too.

Dialog 3   **: Asking name.**

Jack	: Excuse me, what's your name?
Linda	: My name is Linda. What's yours?
Jack	: Jack.
Linda	: You speak English very well.
Jack	: Thank you.
Linda	: Do you know what time it is?
Jack	: Sure. It's 5:10PM.
Linda	: What did you say?
Jack	: I said its 5:10PM.
Linda	: Thanks.
Jack	: You are welcome.

Dialog 4   **: Asking Directions.**

Linda	: Hi Jack.
Jack	: Hi Linda. What's up?
Linda	: I'm looking for the airport. Can you tell me how to get there?
Jack	: No, sorry. I don't know.

Linda	: I think I can take the subway to the airport. Do you know where the subway is?
Jack	: Sure, it's over there.
Linda	: Where? I don't see it.
Jack	: Across the street.
Linda	: Oh, I see it now. Thanks.
Jack	: No problem.
Linda	: Do you know if there's a restroom around here?
Jack	: Yes, there's one here. It's in the store.
Linda	: Thank you.
Jack	: Bye.
Linda	: Bye bye.

Dialog 5   : I'm hurry.

Jack	: Hi Linda, how are you?
Linda	: Fine, how are you doing?
Jack	: OK.
Linda	: What do you want to do?
Jack	: I'm hungry. I'd like to eat something.
Linda	: Where do you want to go?
Jack	: I'd like to go to an Italian restaurant.
Linda	: What kind of Italian food do you like?
Jack	: I like spaghetti. Do you like spaghetti?

Linda   : No, I don't, but I like pizza.

Dialog 6   : Do you want something to drink?

Linda   : Jack, would you like something to eat?

Jack   : No, I'm full.

Linda   : Do you want something to drink?

Jack   : Yes, I'd like some coffee.

Linda   : Sorry, I don't have any coffee.

Jack   : That's OK. I'll have a glass of water.

Linda   : A small glass, or a big one?

Jack   : Small please.

Linda   : Here you are.

Jack   : Thanks.

Linda   : You're welcome.

Dialog 7   : That's too late.

Jack   : Linda, would you like to get something to eat with me?

Linda   : OK. When?

Jack   : At 10 o'clock.

Linda   : 10 in the morning?

Jack   : No, at night.

Linda	: Sorry, that's too late. I usually go to bed around 10:00PM.
Jack	: OK, how about 1:30PM?
Linda	: No, that's too early. I'll still be at work then.
Jack	: How about 5:00PM?
Linda	: OK, see you then.
Jack	: Alright. Bye.

Dialog 8   **: Choosing a time to meet.**

Jack	: Linda, would you like to have dinner with me?
Linda	: Yes. That would be nice. When do you want to go?
Jack	: Is today OK?
Linda	: Sorry, I can't go today.
Jack	: How about tomorrow night?
Linda	: OK. What time?
Jack	: Is 9:00PM all right?
Linda	: I think that's too late.
Jack	: Is 6:00PM OK?
Linda	: Yes, that's good. Where would you like to go?
Jack	: The Italian restaurant on 5th street.
Linda	: Oh, I don't like that restaurant. I don't want to go there.
Jack	: How about the Korean restaurant next to it?
Linda	: OK, I like that place.

Dialog 9 : **When do you want to go?**

Linda   : Hi Jack.

Jack   : Hi.

Linda   : What are you planning to do today?

Jack   : I'm not sure yet.

Linda   : Would you like to have lunch with me.

Jack   : Yes. When?

Linda   : Is 11:30AM OK?

Jack   : Sorry, I didn't hear you. Can you say that again please?

Linda   : I said 11:30AM.

Jack   : Oh, I'm busy then. Can we meet a little later?

Linda   : OK, how about 12:30PM?

Jack   : OK. Where?

Linda   : How about Bill's Seafood Restaurant?

Jack   : Oh, where is that?

Linda   : It's on 7th street.

Jack   : OK, I'll meet you there.

Dialog 10   **: Ordering food.**

Host   : Hello sir, welcome to the French Garden Restaurant. How many?

Jack   : One.

Host   : Right this way. Please have a seat. Your waitress will be with you in a moment.

Waitress : Hello sir, would you like to order now?

Jack   : Yes please.

Waitress : What would you like to drink?

Jack   : What do you have?

Waitress : We have bottled water, juice and Coke.

Jack   : I'll have a bottle of water please.

Waitress : What would you like to eat?

Jack   : I'll have a tuna fish sandwich and a bowl of vegetable soup.

Dialog 11   **: Would you like to go now or later?**

Linda   : Jack, where are you going?

Jack   : I'm going to the store. I need to buy something.

Linda   : Really? I need to go to the store too.

Jack   : Would you like to come with me?

Linda   : Yeah, let's go together.

Jack   : Would you like to go now or later?

Linda   : Now.

Jack	: What?
Linda	: Now would be better.
Jack	: OK, let's go.
Linda	: Should we walk?
Jack	: No, it's too far. Let's drive.

Dialog 12   **: Do you have enough money?**

Jack	: Linda, what are you going to do today?
Linda	: I'm going shopping.
Jack	: What time are you leaving?
Linda	: I'm going to leave around 4 O'clock.
Jack	: Will you buy a ham sandwich for me at the store?
Linda	: OK.
Jack	: Do you have enough money?
Linda	: I'm not sure.
Jack	: How much do you have?
Linda	: 25 dollars. Do you think that's enough?
Jack	: That's not very much.
Linda	: I think it's OK. I also have two credit cards.
Jack	: Let me give you another ten dollars.
Linda	: Thanks. See you later.
Jack	: Bye.

Dialog 13   : **How have you been?**

Linda   : Hello Jack.

Jack   : Hi Linda.

Linda   : How have you been?

Jack   : Not too good.

Linda   : Why?

Jack   : I'm sick.

Linda   : Sorry to hear that.

Jack   : It's OK. It's not serious.

Linda   : That's good. How's your wife?

Jack   : She's good.

Linda   : Is she in America now?

Jack   : No, she's not here yet.

Linda   : Where is she?

Jack   : She's in Canada with our kids.

Linda   : I see. I have to go now. Please tell your wife I said hi.

Jack   : OK, I'll talk to you later.

Linda   : I hope you feel better.

Jack   : Thanks.

Dialog 14   : Introducing a friend.

Linda   : Jack, this is my friend, John.

Jack   : Hi, nice to meet you.

John   : Nice to meet you too.

Jack   : John, what do you do for work?

John   : I'm a doctor.

Jack   : Oh. Where do you work?

John   : New York University hospital in New York City. What do you do?

Jack   : I'm a teacher.

John   : What do you teach?

Jack   : I teach English.

John   : Where?

Jack   : At a high school in New Jersey.

John   : That's nice. How old are you?

Jack   : I'm 30.

Dialog 15   : Buying a shirt.

Jack   : Excuse me.

Linda   : Hello sir, may I help you?

Jack   : Yes. Can I see that shirt on the top shelf please?

Linda   : Sure. Here it is.

Jack	: How much does it cost?
Linda	: 50 dollars.
Jack	: 50 dollars? That's too much.
Linda	: How about this one? It's on sale for only 35 dollars.
Jack	: I don't like that one.
Linda	: How about the one next to the black gloves? It's very 'similar to the one you like.
Jack	: That's nice. How much is it?
Linda	: 30 dollars.
Jack	: That'll be fine.
Linda	: Is this color OK, or would you like a different color?
Jack	: That blue one's fine.
Linda	: Do you need any more of these shirts?
Jack	: Yes.
Linda	: How many do you want?
Jack	: I'll take two more, a red one and a white one.

Dialog 16   : Asking about location.

Jack	: Excuse me; I'm looking for the Holiday Inn. Do you know where it is?
Linda	: Sure. It's down this street on the left.
Jack	: Is it far from here?
Linda	: No, it's not far.
Jack	: How far is it?

Linda	: About a mile and half.
Jack	: How long does it take to get there?
Linda	: 5 minutes or so.
Jack	: Is it close to the subway station?
Linda	: Yes, it's very close. The subway station is next to the hotel. You can walk there.
Jack	: Thanks a lot.

Dialog 17   **: Do you know the address?**

Jack	: Excuse me. Do you know how to get to the mall?
Linda	: Sure, I used to work there. Go straight for about a mile, and then turn left at the light.
Jack	: Do you know the address?
Linda	: Yes, the address is 541, Main Street.
Jack	: Can you write it down for me please?
Linda	: No problem.
Jack	: Is it faster if I take Highland Avenue?
Linda	: No, that way is longer.
Jack	: I think you're right. Thank you.

Dialog 18   **: Vacation to Canada.**

Jack   : What's today's date?

Linda   : It's July 5th.

Jack   : When are you going on vacation?

Linda   : I'm leaving on Sunday. We're going to Canada.

Jack   : Really? The day after tomorrow? That's very soon.

Linda   : Yeah I know.

Jack   : How long are you going to stay there?

Linda   : About 2 weeks.

Jack   : When are you coming back?

Linda   : I'm coming back on the 17th.

Jack   : Alright. Have a nice trip.

Dialog 19   **: Who is that woman?**

Linda   : Jack, who is that woman?

Jack   : That's Jessica.

Linda   : What does she do for work?

Jack   : She's a lawyer.

Linda   : Is she American?

Jack   : No, but she speaks English fluently.

Linda   : She's really tall. Do you know her?

Jack	: Yes, I know her. We're friends.
Linda	: Who's that man standing next to her?
Jack	: Which man?
Linda	: That short guy on her right. What's his name?
Jack	: Oh, that's John.
Linda	: He's really good looking.
Jack	: Yeah.
Linda	: Do you know him?
Jack	: I don't know him, but I think my sister does.
Linda	: Is he married?
Jack	: Yes, he's married.
Linda	: I remember now. I met him before.

Dialog 20 : **Common questions.**

Linda	: Jack, do you know how to speak English?
Jack	: Yes.
Linda	: Where did you learn?
Jack	: I learned in college.
Linda	: You speak really well.
Jack	: Thank you.
Linda	: How long have you been in the US?
Jack	: 3 weeks.

Linda	: Is your wife with you?
Jack	: Yes, she just got here yesterday.
Linda	: Have you been to California before?
Jack	: No, I've never been there.
Linda	: Have you ever been to Las Vegas?
Jack	: Yes. I went there once on a business trip.

Dialog 21   **: The supermarket is closed.**

Linda	: Jack, I'm going to the supermarket. Do you want to come with me?
Jack	: I think the supermarket is closed now.
Linda	: Oh, When does it close?
Jack	: It closes at 7:00 on Sundays.
Linda	: That's too bad.
Jack	: Don't worry, we can go tomorrow morning. It opens at 8:00.
Linda	: Alright. What do you want to do now?
Jack	: Let's take a walk for a half an hour. My sister will get here at about 8:30PM and then we can all go out dinner.
Linda	: Where does she live?
Jack	: She lives in San Francisco.
Linda	: How long has she lived there?
Jack	: I think she's lived there for about 10 years.
Linda	: That's a long time. Where did she live before that?
Jack	: San Diego.

Dialog 22 : **Do you have any children?**

Linda : Jack, do you have any children?

Jack : Yes.

Linda : How many children do you have?

Jack : I have two kids. A boy and a girl.

Linda : What are their names?

Jack : John and Jessica.

Linda : How old are they?

Jack : Jessica is 19 and John is 25.

Linda : Are they in school?

Jack : Jessica is. She goes to college in Washington and John works in Florida.

Linda : What does Jessica study?

Jack : She studies English.

Linda : Is she here now?

Jack : No, she's at school.

Dialog 23 : **Help with pronunciation.**

Linda : Jack, do you like studying English?

Jack : I like studying English, and I can read well. But speaking can be difficult.

Linda : It's not that bad. If you talk to your American friends every day, you'll learn quickly.

Jack : Can I ask you a question?

Linda	: Sure, what do you want to know?
Jack	: I have my book from class here. How do you say this word?
Linda	: Laptop.
Jack	: Sorry, I don't understand. What does that mean?
Linda	: A laptop is a type of computer that you can carry with you. Do you understand?
Jack	: Yes, I think so. Can you say it again?
Linda	: Laptop.
Jack	: Laptop. Did I pronounce that correctly?
Linda	: Yes, that's right. That's very good.
Jack	: Thanks. And this word? How do you pronounce this?
Linda	: That word is pronounced kitchen.
Jack	: Thanks so much. You're a good teacher.
Linda	: Thanks.

Dialog 24   : I lost my wallet.

Jack	: Hey, how's it going?
Linda	: Not good. I lost my wallet.
Jack	: Oh, that's too bad. Was it stolen?
Linda	: No, I think it came out of my pocket when I was in the taxi.
Jack	: Is there anything I can do?
Linda	: Can I borrow some money?
Jack	: Sure, how much do you need?

Linda	: About 50 dollars.
Jack	: That's no problem.
Linda	: Thanks. I'll pay you back on Friday.
Jack	: That'll be fine. Here you are.
Linda	: What are you going to do now?
Jack	: I'm going to buy some books and then I'm going to the gas station.
Linda	: If you wait a minute I can go with you.
Jack	: OK. I'll wait for you.

Dialog 25   **: Phone call at work.**

Jack	: Hello.
Linda	: Hi, is Jack there please?
Jack	: Yes. Who's calling?
Linda	: Linda.
Jack	: One moment please.
Linda	: OK.
Jack	: Hello.
Linda	: Hi Jack, its Linda.
Jack	: Hi Linda.
Linda	: What are you doing now?
Jack	: I'm working.
Linda	: Are you busy?

Jack	: Yes. It's been really busy here all day.
Linda	: What time do you get off of work?
Jack	: 8.00PM.
Linda	: I'll call you back after 8:00PM.
Jack	: OK. Talk to you later.
Linda	: Bye bye.

Dialog 26   : Family trip.

Linda	: Jack, what have you been up to lately?
Jack	: I went on a trip with my family last week.
Linda	: Really? Where did you go?
Jack	: We went to Europe.
Linda	: What cities did you go to?
Jack	: London, Paris and a few other cities.
Linda	: Did you go to Berlin?
Jack	: No, we didn't go there. I'd like to go there next time.
Linda	: I think the summer is a good time to visit Berlin. It's a beautiful place and the people there are very nice.
Jack	: That's what I've heard.
Linda	: I went there last year. If you want, I can give you some information I have about the city.
Jack	: Thanks.

Dialog 27 : **I went shopping.**

Jack : Linda, what did you do today?

Linda : I went shopping.

Jack : Did you buy anything?

Linda : Yes, I bought a few things.

Jack : What did you buy?

Linda : I bought this coat. Do you like it?

Jack : Yeah, I like it a lot. It's very pretty. Where did you buy it?

Linda : At the mall on 6th street.

Jack : Was it expensive?

Linda : No. it wasn't expensive. It was on sale for 20 dollars.

Jack : That's cheap.

Linda : I know. It was a really good deal.

Jack : I don't think you'll need to wear it for a while. It's been really hot lately.

Dialog 28 : **What kind of music do you like?**

Linda : Jack, what kind of music do you like to listen to?

Jack : All kinds, but mostly Pop, rock and classical. Why?

Linda : I have tickets to a show. Do you want to go with me?

Jack : What kind of music is it?

Linda : Pop. It's Mariah Carey.

Jack	: When is it?
Linda	: At 8:00PM tomorrow night.
Jack	: Yeah, I'd like to go. Do you think we should have dinner first?
Linda	: Yes, that's a good idea.
Jack	: Let's eat at the restaurant across the street from my apartment.
Linda	: Oh, I think I know the place you mean. We ate there last month, right?
Jack	: Yes, that's right. You have a good memory.

Dialog 29   **: Going to the library.**

Jack	: Linda, would you like to go to the library with me?
Linda	: OK. Do you think we can go buy a newspaper first?
Jack	: Sure. First we'll go buy a newspaper and then we'll go to the library.
Linda	: Are we going to walk or drive?
Jack	: The weather is really nice today. Let's walk.
Linda	: The weather is good now, but I think it's supposed to rain this afternoon.
Jack	: Alright, then let's take an umbrella. Is your brother coming with us?
Linda	: No, he's still sleeping.
Jack	: Wow, it's already 10:00AM. He must have been up late night.
Linda	: Yeah, he didn't come home until 12:00AM.
Jack	: I hope he can come later.
Linda	: I hope so too. I'll give him a call when we get there.
Jack	: How do we get to the library from here?

Linda   : It's straight down this road on the left, next to the museum. It takes about 10 minutes.

Dialog 30   **: Where do your parents live?**

Jack   : Hi Linda, are you going home this weekend?

Linda   : No, not this weekend. I have too much work to do.

Jack   : Where do your parents live?

Linda   : My father lives in Washington DC.

Jack   : How about your mother?

Linda   : My mother died two years ago.

Jack   : Oh, I am sorry to hear that. Is your father still working?

Linda   : No, he's retired.

Jack   : Do you have any family here?

Linda   : Yes, two of my cousins live here and my aunt and uncle live about 30 miles from here.

Jack   : Do you have any brothers or sisters?

Linda   : Yes, I have two brothers who live in New York and a sister who lives in Boston.

Jack   : Do you see them a lot?

Linda   : Not as much as I'd like to. Usually just on holidays like Thanksgiving and Christmas.

Dialog 31   : Can you help me find a few things?

Jack   : I can't find my glasses and I can't see anything. Can you help me find a few things?

Linda   : No problem. What are you looking for?

Jack   : My laptop, do you see it?

Linda   : Yes, your laptop is on the chair.

Jack   : Where's my book?

Linda   : Which one?

Jack   : The dictionary.

Linda   : It's under the table.

Jack   : Where's my pencil?

Linda   : There's a pencil in front of the lamp.

Jack   : That's not a pencil. That's a pen.

Linda   : Oh, sorry. There is a pencil behind the cup.

Jack   : How about my backpack? Do you know where that is?

Linda   : It's in between the wall and the bed.

Jack   : Where are my shoes?

Linda   : They're on the left side of the TV.

Jack   : I don't see them.

Linda   : Sorry, I made a mistake. They're on the right side of the TV.

Jack   : Thanks.

Linda   : Oh. And here are your glasses. They were next to your cell phone.

Dialog 32   **: Paying for dinner.**

Jack   : Excuse me. Check please.

Waitress   : OK, how was everything?

Jack   : Very nice. Thank you.

Waitress   : Would you like this to-go?

Jack   : Yes, can you put it in a plastic bag?

Waitress   : Sure, no problem. Here you are. That'll be 30 dollars.

Jack   : Do you take credit cards?

Waitress   : Yes, we accept Visa and Master card.

Jack   : OK, here you are.

Waitress   : Thanks. I'll be right back.

Jack   : OK.

Waitress   : Here's your receipt.

Jack   : Thank you.

Waitress   : You're welcome. Please come again.

Dialog 33   **: Buying a plane ticket.**

Man   : Next please. Hello. How can I help you?

Linda   : I'd like to buy a ticket to New York.

Man   : Would you like one way or round trip?

Linda   : Round trip.

Man	: When will you be leaving?
Linda	: When does the next plane leave?
Man	: In about 2 hours.
Linda	: I'd like a ticket for that flight please.
Man	: First class or coach?
Linda	: Coach.
Man	: OK, let me check availability. I'm sorry. Tickets for that flight are sold out.
Linda	: How about the one after that?
Man	: Let me see. Yes, that one still has seats available. Would you like me to reserve a seat for you?
Linda	: Yes, please.
Man	: That'll be 130 dollars.
Linda	: OK.
Man	: Thank you, here's your change.

Dialog 34   : Putting things in order.

Jack	: Linda, can you help me clean things up before we go?
Linda	: Sure. Where should I put this cup?
Jack	: Which cup?
Linda	: The red one.
Jack	: Put it on top of the table.
Linda	: How about this fruit?
Jack	: Oh, that goes in the refrigerator.

Linda	: And those pencils? What should I do with them?
Jack	: Bring those upstairs and put them in the bedroom.
Linda	: How about this pen?
Jack	: Give it to me. I need to use it.
Linda	: What do you want me to do with that paper over there?
Jack	: You can throw that away. I don't need it anymore.
Linda	: The trash is full.
Jack	: Alright, then please put it in a bag and take it outside.
Linda	: OK. Now what?
Jack	: I think we're finished. Can you please turn off the lights and shut the door?
Linda	: Sure.

Dialog 35   **: At the restaurant.**

Linda	: This looks like a nice restaurant.
Jack	: Yeah, it is. I come here all the time.
Linda	: Let's sit over there.
Jack	: OK.
Linda	: Can you pass me a menu please.
Jack	: Sure. What are you going to have to drink?
Linda	: I'm going to have a glass of beer. How about you?
Jack	: I think I'll have a glass of wine.
Linda	: Do you want to order an appetizer first?

Jack	: Not really, maybe we can just order some bread.
Linda	: OK. What are you going to have to eat?
Jack	: I'm not sure. I haven't decided yet. Can you recommend something?
Linda	: Sure, I've had the steak and the lobster before. They're both very good.
Jack	: I think I'll have the lobster. What are you going to have?
Linda	: I'm not that hungry. I think I'm just going to have a salad.
Jack	: I'm gonna go to the bathroom. When the waitress comes back, will you order for me?
Linda	: Sure. No problem.

Dialog 36 : **I need to do laundry.**

Jack	: Hi Linda, come in.
Linda	: Wow, your apartment is a mess.
Jack	: I know. I didn't have time to put things away before you got here.
Linda	: Look! Are those all your clothes on the couch?
Jack	: Yes.
Linda	: Are they clean?
Jack	: Actually most of them are dirty. I haven't done laundry in a while. I usually wait until can do it at my parent's house.
Linda	: My sister and I usually go to the Laundromat down the street. Why don't you go there?
Jack	: I know I should, but that place isn't very convenient. You have to wait for a long time.
Linda	: Yes I know. I have to do it every week. Anyway, are you ready to go?

Jack	: No, I'm not ready yet. I still have to brush my teeth and wash my face. Can you wait for a few minutes?
Linda	: OK, but please hurry. I think the restaurant is closing soon.

Dialog 37   **: Finding a convenient store.**

Jack	: Linda, where's the closest ATM?
Linda	: It's not that far. Do you see that yellow building over there?
Jack	: The big one or the small one?
Linda	: The big one.
Jack	: Yes.
Linda	: It's right next to it, on the right.
Jack	: Do you know if there's a convenience store around here?
Linda	: I don't think there's one around here. The closest one is on 4th street, but that's probably closed now.
Jack	: I really need to get some things before I leave.
Linda	: Well, you could go down to 22nd street. There are lots of stores down there. They are open 24 hours a day.
Jack	: Can I take the subway to get there?
Linda	: Yes, but that'll probably take about half an hour. You should take a cab.
Jack	: Won't that be expensive?
Linda	: No, from here I think it's only about 5 dollars.

Dialog 38 : **Geography and direction.**

Linda : Jack, where's Canada?

Jack : Canada is north of here.

Linda : Can you show me on the map?

Jack : Sure. Look here. Canada is north of the United States.

Linda : Oh, I see. Where's Mexico?

Jack : Mexico is south of the United States.

Linda : How about Connecticut? Where's that?

Jack : Connecticut is east of New York.

Linda : What state is west of Pennsylvania?

Jack : Ohio.

Linda : OK, where's Los Angeles?

Jack : Los Angeles is in California. It's southeast of San Francisco.

Linda : Where's Boston?

Jack : Boston is in the northeast part of the country.

Linda : Where is Las Vegas?

Jack : Las Vegas is in the southwest.

Dialog 39 : **I ate at the hotel.**

Jack : Hi Linda, did you have breakfast yet?

Linda : Yes, I ate at the hotel with my son and my husband.

Jack	: Oh, they have good food there? What did you have?
Linda	: I had some cereal, fried eggs and orange juice.
Jack	: How was it?
Linda	: The food didn't taste very good, and actually I don't feel very well now.
Jack	: That's too bad. Do you want to take a break?
Linda	: No. I'm going to go back to the hotel at lunch time to lie down.
Jack	: OK. I'm going to the drug store later. Is there anything I can get for you?
Linda	: No, that's OK. I think if I rest for a while I'll feel better.

Dialog 40   **: Going to the movies.**

Jack	: Linda, what do you want to do tonight?
Linda	: I'd like to see a movie.
Jack	: I heard Titanic is playing at the movie theater.
Linda	: Oh, I've heard that's a good movie. What time does it start?
Jack	: 6:00PM. It's along movie. I think it lasts for about 3 hours.
Linda	: Will you come and pick me up?
Jack	: What time?
Linda	: I think we should get there early because they might be sold out. Is 5:00PM OK?
Jack	: Yes, that'll be fine. I'll meet you at your house at 5:00PM.
Linda	: Do you want to get something to eat before the movie?
Jack	: I'm not sure there will be enough time for that. We can have popcorn and hotdogs at the theater if you want.

Linda	: I don't like the popcorn they have there. I think they put too much salt on it.
Jack	: OK then, I'll pick you up a little earlier and we can go to the Thai restaurant next to the theater, is that OK?
Linda	: Yes, I like that place.

Dialog 41   **: The food tastes really great.**

Jack	: How do you like the food?
Linda	: It tastes really great. Did you cook it?
Jack	: Yes. I made it this afternoon. Would you like some more?
Linda	: OK, just a little though. I'm really full.
Jack	: Oh. Would you like some soup instead?
Linda	: What kind is it?
Jack	: Tomato and rice. Have you had that before?
Linda	: No. This is my first time. How does it taste?
Jack	: It's good, try it. What do you think?
Linda	: Wow. It is good. Did you make that also?
Jack	: Yes.
Linda	: You're a really good cook.
Jack	: Thanks, next time I'll make chicken soup for us.
Linda	: That sounds good. Did you study cooking in school?
Jack	: No, I learned by myself. I have a good cook book that I read when I have time.

Dialog 42   : Helping a friend move.

Jack   : Linda, will you help me take these things to the car?

Linda   : OK, which car do you want me to put them in?

Jack   : Bring them to my wife's car.

Linda   : Which one is hers?

Jack   : The blue SUV in front of the Honda.

Linda   : What should I take first?

Jack   : That chair over there, but please be careful with it. It was a gift from my mother-in-law.

Linda   : Don't worry, I won't drop it. Wow, it's really heavy. I don't think I can move it by myself.

Jack   : Let me help you with that. I don't want you to hurt your back.

Linda   : Where are you taking all this stuff?

Jack   : Didn't I tell you? We're moving to Florida.

Linda   : You're moving now? I knew you were moving, but I thought you said you were moving next month.

Jack   : Yes, that's true. But my wife found a new apartment on the internet the other day and she wants to move right away.

Dialog 43   : Visiting family.

Jack   : Linda, your husband has a really nice car.

Linda   : Thanks. It's a lot better than mine, and it's new.

Jack   : Where are you going?

Linda	: We're going to visit my sister in the city.
Jack	: I didn't know your sister lives in the city. When did she move there?
Linda	: About a year ago. She lives in an apartment on 4th street, across from the public library.
Jack	: I see. It's almost 5:00PM now. Don't you think there will be a lot of traffic?
Linda	: Oh, we're not driving. We're going to take the subway. The subway only takes about 20 minutes.
Jack	: Yes, but it can be very crowded around this time. I always feel uncomfortable taking the subway.
Linda	: I take the subway to work every day. So, I'm used to it now.
Jack	: Doesn't your mother live in the city?
Linda	: Yes, she's lived there for about ten years.
Jack	: I remember when she moved there. Apartments were a lot cheaper then.
Linda	: I know what you mean. It's hard to find anything that's reasonable now.
Jack	: Have a good time. Next time you're free, give me a call and we'll go play poker.
Linda	: See you later.

Dialog 44   : Looking at vacation pictures.

Linda	: Jack, I heard you took a trip to San Diego. Is that right?
Jack	: Yeah, I just got back this morning.
Linda	: That sounds really nice. What did you do there?
Jack	: Well, we were only there for three days. So we didn't do too much. We went shopping and went out to dinner a few times. And at night we walked around the city with some friends.

Linda	: Do you take any pictures?
Jack	: Yes, I have them with me. Do you want to look at them?
Linda	: Sure, I love looking at photos.
Jack	: This one is of my wife and me on the beach, and this one is our daughter Anne standing next to my wife.
Linda	: Your daughter looks like her mother.
Jack	: I know. they look very similar.
Linda	: Where was this picture taken?
Jack	: That was taken at the train station before we left.
Linda	: Did you have time to go to the zoo?
Jack	: No, not this time. We went there last time.
Linda	: It looks like you all had a nice time.
Jack	: Yeah, it was a lot of fun.

Dialog 45 : **Ordering some flowers.**

Woman	: Good afternoon, how may I help you?
Jack	: Hi, I'd like to order some flowers.
Woman	: Who are they for?
Jack	: They're for my wife. Her name is Linda.
Woman	: What kind of flowers would you like?
Jack	: I don't know. I don't know too much about flowers. Can you recommend something?
Woman	: OK. What's the reason you are sending her flowers.

Jack	: Today's her birthday and she told me she wants me to buy her flowers.
Woman	: Do you know what kind of flowers she likes?
Jack	: I'm not sure. I know I should know that, but I can't remember right now.
Woman	: Well, they're for your wife, so I think you should give her roses.
Jack	: Roses will be fine.
Woman	: What color?
Jack	: I think red would be nice.
Woman	: Do you want to pick them up or should we deliver them?
Jack	: Can you deliver them please?
Woman	: What's the address?
Jack	: 345, Main Street.
Linda	: Alright, they'll be there within two hours.

Dialog 46   **: Leaving a message.**

Linda	: Hello?
Jack	: Hi, is Anne there please?
Linda	: Sorry, I think you have the wrong number.
Jack	: Is this 617-329-3312?
Linda	: Yes. Who are you looking for again?
Jack	: Anne Smith.
Linda	: Oh, I thought you said Anny. Sorry about that. This is the right number, but Anne's not here right now.
Jack	: Do you know where she went?

Linda	: She went to the store to buy some groceries. Would you like to leave a message?
Jack	: Yes, would you please tell her Jack called?
Linda	: Hi Jack, this is her roommate Linda. I met you a couple months ago at the Christmas party.
Jack	: Oh, yes. How are you?
Linda	: Good. Anne will be back in about 30 minutes. I'll tell her you called.
Jack	: OK. Thanks.
Linda	: Bye bye.

Dialog 47 : Talking about weather.

Linda	: Hello?
Jack	: Hi Linda, its Jack.
Linda	: Hi Jack.
Jack	: How's the weather there today?
Linda	: It's really cold. It snowed all day and the schools closed early.
Jack	: What's the temperature?
Linda	: its 30 degrees now. It was even colder this morning.
Jack	: Have you heard what the weather is going to be like tomorrow?
Linda	: I was watching the news a little earlier. They said it's probably going to snow tomorrow.
Jack	: I really don't like the winter. I wish it were summer.
Linda	: Me too. How's the weather where you are?

Jack : It's not too bad, but it's pretty cold here too. It was about 45 today and it rained this afternoon. I heard it's going to be a little warmer tomorrow.

Dialog 48 : **Making plans.**

Jack : It's almost Christmas. What are you doing this weekend?

Linda : Nothing special, just working. Why do you ask?

Jack : Well, I still haven't finished my Christmas shopping. Do you want to go shopping with me this weekend?

Linda : I'd like to, but I'm not sure if I can. Work has been really busy lately. Why don't we go on Friday instead?

Jack : Friday's not good. I think the stores will be very crowded and I have to work.

Linda : OK, then let's try to go this weekend. I should know if I can go by Friday. Is it OK if I call you then?

Jack : Yeah, that's fine.

Linda : What's your number?

Jack : 234-543-9768. Let me give you my email address too. It's jack@gmail.com

Linda : OK, I'll talk to you soon.

Jack : OK.

Dialog 49 : **Meeting a friend.**

Jack : Hello?

Linda : Hi Jack.

Jack	: Are you there yet?
Linda	: Yes.
Jack	: I just got off the subway. I'm almost there. Sorry I'm late.
Linda	: That's no problem. I just wanted to tell you I'm inside.
Jack	: Where are you?
Linda	: On the second floor.
Jack	: Should I come to the second floor or do you want to come to the first floor?
Linda	: Come upstairs.
Jack	: What?
Linda	: Oh, can you hear me? I said, come to the second floor.
Jack	: Oh, OK. What are you doing there?
Linda	: Just looking at some books on how to learn English.
Jack	: Do you want to get something to eat later?
Linda	: No, I'm still full from dinner.
Jack	: What do you want to do?
Linda	: I don't know for sure. When you get here we'll talk about it.
Jack	: OK, see you soon.
Linda	: Bye.

Dialog 50   : I'm a student.

Jack	: Linda, what do you do for work?
Linda	: I'm still a student.

Jack	: What school do you go to?
Linda	: Mississippi State University.
Jack	: That's a good school. What do you study?
Linda	: I'm studying English, math and history. My major is English.
Jack	: How long have you been studying English?
Linda	: More than six years.
Jack	: That's a long time.
Linda	: Yeah, I started to learn English when I was in high school.
Jack	: No wonder your English is so good.
Linda	: Actually, it's not that good. I can read but I can't speak very well. I haven't had a lot of chance to practice.
Jack	: I see. Talking with other people is very important.
Linda	: Yes, but I still don't have many friends here yet.
Jack	: I'm having a party tonight at my apartment. You should come.
Linda	: Oh thanks for inviting me. I'd love to come.

Speaking Part 2

In this part you will be given a card called Cue card and asks to talk about a particular topic. You will be given 1 minute to prepare before speaking. After that you will have talk about the topic which was given to you for 2 minutes. Do not bother about the time. The examiner will stop you when time exceeds.

Things you should do:

➤ You should take notes while writing keywords.
➤ Remember to cover every point.
➤ Talk point to point. Give a smooth flow.
➤ You can use a personal experience. Or else you can lie. No one knows except you.
➤ You can expand using your senses.
➤ You can organize your speech. For example: introduction, body and conclusion.
➤ Just remember to imagine the object, person or place while you are speaking.
➤ You can use introductory phrases like 'I want to talk about'.
➤ Remember to speak loudly.

Things you shouldn't do:

➤ Don't memorize answers while speaking.
➤ Don't write too much while you taking down notes. Write only 1-2 words per point.
➤ Don't be panic.
➤ Focus on one point while you speak.
➤ Don't you boring words like good, bad. Be smart.
➤ Don't go off topic.
➤ Especially don't worry about your accent. Everybody has an accent. If it is understandable it's okay.

It's necessary to practice as much as possible in this part as well. For that purpose I will give you 60 Cue card examples with answers. Try to relate those answers to you. Practice more. By practicing for one example, you will be able to answer several Cue card topics as well.

Sample Cue Card 1

> # Describe a friend who you really like to spend time with.
>
> **You should say:**
> - ➤ When and how you met
> - ➤ How often you see this friend
> - ➤ What kind of personality your friend has
>
> **And say why you like to spend time with this particular friend.**

Sample Answer 1:

The friend I like to spent time with is Steve. I met him when I was only 8 years old and was in primary school. After that our intimacy grew up and we became best friends. One day he forgot to bring his book in school and that day I helped him with my expire books. After that we talked for a long after school and our friendship started to begin. We went to college together and then got admitted in different Universities. Since we were studying in the same city, we could meet each other and spent time together.

We are yet to finish our graduation and busy with our own stuffs. But whenever we get a vacation we spend time together. Since our hometown is same, we go there together and thus we meet each other at least twice in a month. He is a helpful and talented friend who helps people and always wishes best for people. He is studying Mathematics and he has a talent in Mathematics. Sometimes he explains some complex mathematical theories in a very simple and interesting way. He is passionate about reading books and that makes a good bonding with me. We often exchange our thought and criticism about books and politics.

I like to spend time with him because we have many common interests between us. I never feel bored spending time with him. Since we are friends for a long time, we understand each other. A good friend always extends helping hands when in need and I've found Steve by my side always. We do so many fun stuffs together and help each other in our study. Good friendship, understanding and common interests makes us close friends and those are the major factors for what I like to spend time with his.

Sample Answer 2:

I happened to meet this person who later became my friend in a yoga and meditation class which I joined quite lately. It was quite a chance that this person who goes by the name, Steve, sat beside me during the class. The reason why I like spending time with him is the positive vibes that I feel out of him. He is one of the persons, rather the first person in my life whom I have met having a very positive attitude towards the life.

I always found him in jubilant mood in spite of the fact that he had a very troublesome incident in his life. He lost his only son and that too at a young age of 25. I must say, he is one of the persons who have really made a positive impression on my mind and has contributed a lot in the way I have started looking at life.

After these classes, it has been quite a regular feature that I spend my time in his company, almost every weekend. Yet another reason why I like spending time with Steve is the humorous character that he possesses.

Sample Cue Card 2

Describe a party that you have attended.

You should say:
- ➤ What type of party it was
- ➤ Where the party was held
- ➤ Who attended the party

And describe what you did in that party.

Sample Answer 1:

Today I'm going to tell you about a particular party I went to earlier in this year, I'll tell you where it was, and who went and what I got up to whilst I was there. In honesty I can be a bit grumpy about going to parties. I never know what to wear as I don't really like dressing up. I feel self-conscious in dresses and too much of a scruff if I don't make an effort. I worry about whether I'll know anyone, and I dread sit-down meals because I'm a vegetarian and I always seem to be a problem. This being so, when a close friend of mine announced she would have a big celebration for her fiftieth birthday. My heart sank a bit. Of course I put on a smile, and said 'that's great'. But I wasn't really looking forward to it. I knew that it was important to her though, so I was determined to make a real effort, and of course I agreed I would go.

Well, I should have had more faith. The party was great. It was held in a beautifully converted barn in a rural location on the edges of Sheffield in England. The venue had a wooden polished floor, and was very simply decorated with some tastefully positioned fairy lights and candles. The candles were in fact artificial for safety reasons, but they looked very realistic. There was low-level music playing and lots of places to sit and chat or mingle with other guests. If I remember correctly, there were white table cloths over the tables and some simple but lovely floral decorations. Food was provided by a friend of the Birthday Girl, who specializes in fast street food. You could queue up for a delicious meal presented in a wrap from a very jolly woman serving from an open-sided vehicle parked in the cobbled courtyard outside. In a separate annexed room inside was a table almost collapsing under the weight of delicious home-made cakes and puddings on one side, and glorious British cheeses were on the other. There was also a small bar serving drinks, for which my host picked up the bill at the end. It was really beautifully done, very tasteful, calm and joyful too.

My friend, whose birthday it was, has a really wide network of friends. She decided to invite anyone and everyone from her social circle. So there were old school friends, people she knew from her voluntary activities with scouts, fellow runners – she is very active in a number of running clubs. Former work colleagues, people she'd come to know just from waiting with other parents at the school gates when her children were little, fellow entrepreneurs (*she runs her own small business*) as well as neighbors and acquaintances from every area of her life.

Before I went I was worried about whether I'd know anyone else there. I hadn't been living in the area for all that long before being invited, and so I was a bit hesitant about what to expect. I should have remembered what a good judge of character my fantastically friendly friend is! What did I do at the party? Apart from eating my body weight in delicious food, I met and talked to many interesting people that I might otherwise never have come across. This included the self-employed interior designer, marathon runners, a former Bluebell girl (*that's a famous Parisian dance troupe*), artists, writers, an organ transplant co-coordinator, medical doctors, IT workers, academics and students. It was a remarkable cross section of fascinating folk. I had a really wonderful time.

What's more, I discovered that actually I did know quite a few people there after all. It was great fun trying to discover how we all came to be there and what connected each of us to the –'hostess with the mostest' to coin the old phrase! I am almost won over. Next time she offers to host a party, I might even find myself looking forward to it, you never know.

Sample Answer 2:

The party I'd like to describe is the New Year eve party that I attended 2 years back. Our University friends invited me to join the party and I had to contribute some amount for that. The party held on a 3 star hotel where the teachers, students and their relatives attended.

On the New Year eve one of my friends gave me a call and then I picked up a taxi to reach the hotel. The name of the hotel was (*say a hotel name you prefer*) and it was a beautiful hotel in our city. After I reach the hotel I found that it has been gorgeously decorated with lights. Our party was in the 2nd floor and I found most of my friends and some of the teachers already enjoying the party.

A local music band was singing and people were wearing mostly party dresses. We enjoyed the party a lot and ate several local and foreign dishes. We started counting down the time at 11:59 pm and when the clock ticked at 12:00, we started shouting with the New Year wishes. We stayed at the party till 2.00 am and all those time we enjoyed our time every way possible.

Sample Cue Card 3

> # Describe a museum that you have visited.
>
> **You should say:**
> - ➤ When you visited the museum
> - ➤ Describe the museum
> - ➤ How you felt after going there
>
> **And describe your experience of the visit.**

Sample Answer:

I have visited 3-4 museums in total in different countries and enjoyed visiting the (*tell a museum name you know about*) in (*say the country name*). I went to the museum 2 years back while visiting the city. Visiting the museum was not in our tour plan and yet we went there as it was prominently expressing its present in front of us. I went there with my 2 friends and one cousin who were my tour partners. My cousin and one of my friends were not at all interested to roam inside the museum as they had other plans. I insisted them to go there and I convinced them by saying that if you do not enjoy it I would pay for the dinner.

After we bought our tickets, we entered in to the museum and the colossal front side of the museum building and the large open garden in front of it mesmerized us. At that time I had a feeling that our time would worth the visit.

After we entered inside the museum, we found that the place is even larger than we initially thought it would be. There were 5 floors in the museum and the inside architecture reminded us the imperial age. We could see the top of the building from the ground flood. People from different age groups and countries were closely observing the museum. Taking photo was prohibited and yet I was sometimes allured to take some hidden snaps especially when I saw the colossal dinosaur fossil and alien ship.

The first floor of the museum had some art from famous artist of the world and sculptures from different era. The first floor gave us the impression of visiting a theatre or art gallery rather than museum. We came to know that some of the arts were so expensive that one can buy an island by selling it! Then we moved to the second floor which was full of Second World War memories. Guns, tanks and other war materials from 1945 WW II had been arranged there. A video was showing some of the fighting scenes of WW II.

When we reached third floor, it's been already 2.5 hours. We found all the costumes and traditional things from different parts of the world have been placed here. One can easily learn about the customs of different ages and countries just by visiting this floor. The next floor had more adventure and surprises for us. It has placed all the major inventions of different ages and they were historically famous. I felt overwhelmed seeing the First computer, Speed boat, Wheel, Motor Engine and many more famous invention of history at this floor. I was so much dying to touch the first 4 wheeler that had been placed there.

We had visited the whole museum as much as possible and spent almost the whole day. We were so enthralled to visit the place that we literally forgot to have our lunch. The overall experience was fantastic and I learned so many things in few hours. As soon as I left the place, I planned to revisit it someday.

Sample Cue Card 4

Describe a happy event of your life.

You should say:
- What it was
- When it happened
- Where it happened

And explain why it was a happy event.

Sample Answer 1:

I can remember many happy events of my life and out of those I would like to talk about the event that I can still remember vividly regarding my success in the board exam. The moment I heard that I had been awarded a scholarship based on my performance in the board exam, I became the happiest man in the world. This was indeed a very happy moment for me as it is something I was looking forward to achieve and the news made my parents quite happy and proud.

I spent almost a month with great anxiety regarding my result publication. I started speculating so many things and many of them were negative. I could hardly keep away the tensions about my upcoming result. The result was so important that my college admission was depended on it. I could not sleep well in the night before the result publishing. I think this is a common anxiety for students and I was familiar with this type of anxiety. However, this particular exam results gave me more nightmares than any other time of my life.

The result was published at around 10.00 am and I found that I did exceptionally well. I was so relieved and happy that I literally shouted. Then I hurriedly came back to our home and gave the news to my parents. They were happy too. My father bought sweets and my mother gave it to our neighbors. I felt excited, happy and relieved. At that time I was about 15 years old. It happened at our hometown called (*say the name of your home-town*).

Sample Answer 2:

In my face, I feel a glow whenever I remember the day I went to the International trade fair with some of my friends. That was my first International trade fair visit and this was such a happy experience that I still feel a great joy reciting the memory of this event. It was January, 1999 and that time I was in my first year of college.

Till my college I was like a new born lady, who had never visited any places without her places of her local area. After I got admitted in to the college, I started exploring the world and the amazing things that invites people like us. One day I planned with my friends that we would visit International trade fair. This might seem like a very usual and banal event for others but to me that was a really exciting thing to do. Later on we did as we thought and finalized our visit to the fair. After break period at college, we escaped by back door (*As a side note, I would like to mention that I'd no previous record of escaping school or college before*). We were five in members and we hired taxi to reach the trade fair. There wasn't enough space to sit in the back side of the taxi and the taxi driver gave a suspicious look at us. That's why with a fishy smile we took the decision that one of us would sit in front of the baby taxi with the taxi driver. It was a funny decision but there was no alternative to us and we enjoyed it.

After few minutes we reached at the fair and then collected the tickets. We were thoroughly enjoying everything we did that time. We entered the fair and took a deep breath to ease ourselves. We were kind of overwhelmed to observe the vast area with hundreds of shops and stalls. People were all around us and we felt like somehow we have come to a fairy land. Wherever we went, I was feeling so excited, everything was totally new for me as a grown up lady. We took lots of photos from different views, purchased few interesting things within our limited budget and roamed in the whole area of the fair. I forgot my usual area, boundaries and the same thing I do almost every day and felt a happiness that I missed for a long. We spent almost 4-5 hours in the trade fair and at last retuned to our home in the evening. We returned home by bus and I was so happy that I felt like discovering a new continent.

Sample Cue Card 5

Describe a teacher who has influenced you in your education.

You should say:
  ➤ Where you met him/her
  ➤   What subject/s he/she taught
  ➤ What was special about him/her
And explain why this person influenced you so much.

Sample Answer:

I consider myself lucky to get several very good teachers throughout my academic years. Among them I'd like to talk about Mr. Steve who was an extraordinary teacher, a really good mentor and who has a great influence in my education.

I met Mr. Steve when I was in class 4 and he was our math teacher. Initially we thought that he would be a moody teacher and we would have to be very polite in front of him. This impression came mostly because of his serious face and tidy dress-up. But soon we found that, he is a very friendly person and teaches us very well. He never made things complicated and tried over and over again to explain something to us. He had a very unique way of teaching. Seems like he would start an interesting story and later we would find that he would relate the math with the story. Thus everything we learned from him was interesting and that's why we remember most of the theory and techniques of math he taught us.

I'd say he has a great influence in my education because he made a very strong foundation on Mathematics. Later on I studied Science and the Mathematics was the most important subject. I have always been good at math and that mainly because of Mr. Steve who had a major role on making the subject interesting to me. Before I learned math from Mr. Steve, my impression on math was not good and I considered mathematics to be a very difficult and uninteresting subject. But his teaching and influences changed my way of thinking about math and later on math became my one of the most favorite subjects.

Sample Cue Card 6

Describe a historical place that you know about.

You should say:
- ➢ What the place is
- ➢ Where it is located
- ➢ What is the historical significance of the place

And describe your experience of the place.

Sample Answer 1:

I have a special interest on visiting famous places and on my list historical places always get preferences. I have visited many historical places like Machu Picchu in Peru, The Pyramids at Giza, Taj Mahal, Parthenon in Greece and many more. The historical significance and the site attractions sometimes mesmerized me. The historical place that I would like to talk about today is Coliseum which is situated in Rome, Italy. It is basically an elliptical amphitheater in the center of the city of Rome, Italy which is the largest amphitheater in the world and is made of concrete and stone. The construction of Coliseum began under the emperor Vespasian in 70 AD and was completed under Titus in 80 AD.

The Coliseum could hold approximately 50,000 to 80,000 spectators and was used for gladiatorial contests and public spectacles such as mock sea battles, animal hunts, executions, re-enactments of famous battles etc. The Coliseum was listed as a World Heritage Site by UNESCO in 1980 and was also included among the New Seven Wonders of the World. It is 189 meters long, and 156 meters wide, with a base area of 6 acres .The height of the outer wall is 48 meters. The Coliseum nowadays is one of the major tourist attractions in Rome with thousands of tourists each year paying to view the interior arena.

I have heard and seen of this famous place a lot and when I witnessed it for the first time, I became speechless. The huge architect, the overwhelming interior and exterior decoration was beyond appreciation. The place kept reminding me the classical mythological and historical facts I have read and heard about.

Sample Answer 2:

I am going to talk about an amazing historical place that I know about, even though I've never visited it. I'll tell you what it is, where it is and as much as I can about the historical meaning of the place and finally my own reactions/ experiences regarding it.

I want to tell you about Stonehenge. This is an ancient set of standing stones, arranged in a circle. It is located in Wiltshire, in England. But I think it would be fair to say the image of it would be recognized worldwide, as it is possibly one of the most famous historic sites in the world.

In terms of the meaning of the place it's really impossible to say. It is so very old, even archaeologists aren't sure exactly when it was built, estimates go back to as long ago as 3000 BC, which is mind boggling to me! It is certainly accurate to describe it as a prehistoric monument. Some people think it might have started as a burial mound and be even more ancient those 5,000 years. The colossal slabs are arranged like huge door frames, no-one really knows how they were erected without the technology of modern times, but everyone agrees it was an incredible feat of engineering and showed foresight and tenacity in spaces! However, it is certain that they were somehow aligned so that at key stages of the lunar (*moon*) and solar (*sun*) cycles, the way the light strikes the stones is of some significance. Apparently it was deliberately constructed so that the rising sun only reached the middle of the stones for just one day of the year.

Lots of people like to try and imagine what sort of ceremonies and importance the stones might have had for the people who built it, but the truth is we can't say. Even today, modern day druids have for many years gathered at the stones for the summer solstice (*longest day of the year*) and winter solstice (*shortest day of the year*) to watch the sun rise and mark the event with their own celebrations.

For me I think this is the ultimate historical place, even though I have yet to visit it. It is just so remarkable to think it was constructed all those thousands of years ago just by physical labor. Even the stones themselves – the largest of which are up to 30 feet and weigh about 25 tons, had to be brought to the site from about 20 miles away, how on earth was that possible? For me the stones prove that with determination, tenacity and working together it is sometimes possible to achieve what seems impossible. At the same time, the way they have endured over time, gives perspective on our place in the world. Time passes, people and generations pass too, but they can leave a legacy behind even if it only one of many unanswered questions for future people to ponder over.

Sample Cue Card 7

Describe an accident you saw.

You should say:
- Where the accident occurred
- Where you were then
- How the accident affected you

And give detailed information about the accident.

Sample Answer 1:

The most devastating accident that I have ever seen is the one that I witnessed near (*say the name of the place*) while a train smashed a passing bus. I saw accident almost 4 years back and yet I can remember the event clearly. I was on my way to home from the capital city that I'm currently residing in. There is a train pass in the road and our bus stopped at the signal. I was busy reading a magazine in the bus and all of a sudden I heard a loud blasting sound and I looked through the window. What I saw was unbelievable. The quickly passing train has hit a bus that was trying to pass the train road. The bus had been thrown away like a toy and we could hear the unbearable screaming of victims. Lots of people have gathered the place and the train was passing slowly. People became speechless on the effect of the devastating accident. I could see people were trying to help the wounded people and 3-4 ambulances reached there after 15 minutes. The bus driver was blamed for the incident and I heard that he was dead too. We could not move on from the place as a huge jam occurred. The wounded people were moved to nearby hospitals and medical centers and the dead people were placed in a nearby field. The entire place became a gloomy area and people mourned on the event. I started feeling sick and tried to help the wounded people.

I have witnessed more than 30 people were lying dead and their relatives were crying and mourning heavily. I left the place after about 5 hours and could not think anything else. The whole event occurred in a few minutes and the effect was devastating. I had spent nearly 2 weeks in a hallucination and thought a lot about the people who died there and about their relatives. It came to my mind that, our life is hanging on the cliffs and we are so helpless sometimes deciding our fates.

Sample Answer 2:

The idea of an accident sounds like it should be bad. But sometimes accidents are quite comical to watch and if nobody is hurt then I think it is OK to laugh.

I'm going to tell you a story about an accident I saw a very, very long time ago. But I can remember it really well, you'll find out why in a bit. I'll explain where the accident took place, where I was, a bit of detail about the incident and how it affected me.

The accident took place in a large old house that was in very poor repair. I was unemployed at the time, and was sharing the house with a few friends who were also job-seeking as we had all just finished at university. It was in the 1980s and it was very difficult to get work in the UK at that time. We had chosen the house because it was really cheap. The way it was set out wasn't very safe, there was a tiny kitchen on a stair well that we all had to share, and this meant that many of our communal chats took place sitting on the stairs gathered around the landing.

On this particular day it was first thing in the morning. We were all half asleep and stumbling around just in our dressing gowns or nightwear. I was sat at the top of the stairs (*near to the kitchen*) waiting to use the kitchen as one of my friends, Gill, had got in their first and there wasn't room for both of us. Another of our house mates appeared at the bottom of the stairs and sat there looking tearful and crestfallen. She had had a terrible argument with her boyfriend and was very upset. Gill, who was already in the kitchen, kindly offered to make her a cup of tea – but as she was putting the kettle on she was distracted by the tears of our upset mutual friend. Gill turned to talk to her just as she was lighting the gas – catastrophe! The flame caught her dressing gown and the next moment the whole garment seemed on fire. I gasped, my tea-making friend thought quickly, she ripped off her clothes, and rolled on the floor, tumbling down the stairs ending up in a naked heap at the feet of our crying companion. The shock of this sight caused the sobs to stop. '*Why are you at the bottom of the stairs and why have you got no clothes on?*' queried our now no-longer crying friend. I and my friend Gill just laughed uproariously, partly with relief (*it could have been a lot worse*) and partly with disbelief. Our upset friend had been so preoccupied with her own worries she'd missed the entire thing. We couldn't believe it when it was all so dramatic.

How did the accident affect me? It just made me laugh a lot at the time, and even now when I remember it I do so with a smile. It was such a ridiculous thing to happen, and it certainly broke the rather serious mood the morning had started with. I also think we were very lucky, it might not have ended that way. There is a saying that '*all's well that ends well*' – that was certainly the case here.

Perhaps it isn't true to say that no-one was hurt in this story, I think that maybe pride was hurt quite a bit, but it was a long time ago and the main '*victim*' of this story, Gill, still laughs about it with me now.

Sample Answer 3:

Wow, talking about an accident I saw is quite challenging. I can think an example, but it wasn't nice to witness. I'll tell you where the accident occurred and where I was at the time, a bit of extra detail about what happened, and then finally I'll tell you what happened. That seems a logical way to explain it.

The accident took place in the outdoor arena of a large horse riding school, where I was sharing a jumping lesson with a friend. The backdrop to where it took place is really beautiful, as the equestrian center is set in a rural location in the picturesque countryside of Glossop, which is within an area known as the High Peaks in the county of Derbyshire, England.

My friend and I both wanted to improve our technique show jumping. I'm quite an experienced rider, but not very confident jumping – I prefer flat work, my friend is a great athlete, but new to horse riding, she was very confident, but not very experienced. We had warmed up already, riding our horses around under the guidance of an instructor at walk, trot and canter. We'd taken the horses over some low cross-poles, which are small jumps you commonly use when you are teaching either a horse or rider to jump so they can gain confidence. About 15 minutes into the lesson, we started to take it in turns to try slightly bigger fences, but nothing too challenging. I'd already taken my horse over, and it was my friend's turn to try. So I was sat on my horse watching her as she rode towards the fence. The instructor and I were both very calm, as was my friend, it was a small cross pole, and nothing she and the horse hadn't done before.

She trotted her pony to the jump, but then at the last minute, her mount just stumbled, literally tripping over the poles. Perhaps because my friend was a bit inexperienced, it caused her to lose her balance, the teacher and I both gasped, and then laughed as she seemed to recover herself and ended up back in the saddle. Unfortunately, we relaxed too soon, the horse seemed to still have her feet in a knot and so tripped again, this time the forward momentum catapulted my friend into the air. We watched in slow motion as she went up in a huge arc, and then fell towards the ground. Unfortunately, her instinct was to put her hand out to break her fall, this meant her arm was completely extended and she took the full weight of her body onto just one hand. We heard a sickening split as the bones in her lower arm broke, and it was very obvious that she had a serious injury. She was still conscious, but in an awful lot of pain.

You never quite know how you will behave in an accident. I went into very calm mode. I quickly dismounted and caught the loose horse, who was a bit confused about what had happened. The instructor called an ambulance, and I took the horses back to the yard, explained what had happened, and arranged for people to stand at various points on the property to help direct the ambulance to where it was needed before going back to the school. Unfortunately, the instructor was rather squeamish, she couldn't bear the sight of blood and so although she was handling the situation well, she couldn't really look at my friend. So I sat near her and tried to keep her talking while we all waited for the ambulance. We knew it was very important she didn't move in case she had broken her back as well, and we were trying to keep her conscious so it would be possible for the paramedics to assess her more easily when they came.

The ambulance took a very, very long time to arrive because of our remote location. However, when they came they were fantastic. They gave my friend a lot of morphine – which is a very powerful pain killer – and were incredibly calm. I had to help roll her onto the stretcher, but we were very relieved when she went off to hospital safely. Her arm was very badly damaged. She has had lots of operations and I'm not sure if she will be riding again.

The accident affected me quite a lot, because I was astounded that she was so unlucky in how she fell. The horse just tripped, it wasn't being naughty or difficult, and it all happened in slow motion so right up until the last minute I thought she might be alright. I was pleased how well me and the instructor worked together to get help, and that I'd been able to stay calm and focused at the time. Since then I have jumped again, but really I think I've decided to stick to flat work (*dressage*) from now on. Watching an accident makes you realize how fragile life can be and how easily and quickly you can be hurt, not through being stupid, but just through being unlucky.

Sample Cue Card 8

Describe one of your childhood memories.

You should say:
  - ➢ What it is
  - ➢ When it happened
  - ➢ How it affected you in your life

And explain why you still remember it.

Sample Answer 1:

Childhood memories are strange things, because sometimes you can't quite be sure if you really remember something, or if you just think you do because others have told you about it, or you have seen a photo of the event later on. I'm going to talk to you about a memory that I'm very confident is real. I'll tell you what it is, when it happened, how it affected me and why I still remember it.

The memory is the earliest one I have of me and my Dad. I was very small indeed, I'm not exactly sure how old, but I'd guess about three years old, maybe even younger. My Dad was not a particularly tall or strong man, but I was small enough, and by comparison, he was big enough then, for me to stand with both my feet on one of his, and to reach up with my arms and cling onto his leg. I would then hang on and laugh delightedly as he tried to go about his daily business, walking around the house with me gripping on tightly refusing to be budged. It was a favorite game.

I don't know that I can honestly say it affected me in my life. However, in my family we don't really talk about things very much nor do a lot together. We don't live particularly close to one another so see each other rather infrequently. I suppose the way the incident affected me was by making me at a subconscious level feel close to my Dad even years later as we had shared that happy play time together when I was tiny.

I didn't know I had held onto this memory until quite recently. Sadly my Dad died, he had been very ill for a long time, so it wasn't unexpected, but of course it was very sad. I wanted to say something about him at his funeral, and I wanted to pick a memory that was personal just to him and to me. For some reason that image of me tiny and laughing and him solemnly 'pretending' that he hadn't noticed I was there came into my mind and it seemed very appropriate somehow to share that one. It was a happy memory, but also an intimate one. I think he would have been really pleased that I could recall it so many decades later.

So why can I remember it? I'm not sure, but I like to think the memory was there dormant all the time just waiting for the moment when I needed to retrieve it. It is a comforting thing to recall. The human mind is an amazing thing.

Sample Answer 2:

I can still remember lots of thing I did in my childhood and things that happened when I was a child. Sometimes those memories seem so lucid that it seems those events occurred only few days back. Anyway, a childhood memory I can still remember so clearly is the first time when I saw massive death. I was a kid of class three or four then and one day I heard that there had been an accident near our home. My mother asked me whether I want to go or not. I went with her and speculated lots of thing about the accident but when I watched 10 dead people were kept lying in the ground and among them there were 2 kids too, I was devastated about the massive dead scene. I started feeling sick and started vomiting there. My mother took me back to our home and I was ill for about two days.

This memory was important to me because it helped me to think about the life in a different way. I could realize then what the dead is and how fragile our lives are. This memory helped me to grow faster and opened my eyes of vision.

Sample Answer 3:

I was born in a beautiful urban area called (*say your birthplace name*) and the place was full of magic and wonder. I spent my whole childhood there and the place is full with my childhood memories. Childhood is perhaps, the most magical and beautiful time of our life and I cherish my childhood memory. The one particular memory of my childhood I would never forget is the time I first saw the devastating effect of accident. This event has a significant importance of my life.

Like most other newly school going kids, I wanted to be Superman or Spiderman. The life was full of dreams and fantasy. One day I was walking with my mom and heard from the neighbors that a severe accident has happened nearby. I was bit confused what was it all about. Finally I and mom reached at the place where the accident took place. We saw that people had made a crowd around the victims who were already dead. I observed the dead for the first time in my life. We did not stay there for a long. After returning home I felt sick. Later on I started realizing that our lives are fragile and are not eternal. We all will die someday no matter what we think we are. That event helped me growing up mentally. Not that I become pessimist from the event, but a realization always knocked me. I started changing some of my silly attitudes after the event. I started caring for my parents, relatives, known and unknown people. I learned that our days are numbered and we've to make best use of it. I was so deeply touched that I started praying every day and became kind to insects and animals. Some people might think that the event was devastating for a kid, but to me, it revealed reality in front of me.

Sample Cue Card 9

Describe a website you often browse.

You should say:
- ➤ What is it
- ➤ How long have you been using it
- ➤ Give details information about the website

And explain why you often browse this website.

Sample Answer 1:

I have just a few minutes to tell you about a website I often browse. I will tell you what the website is, how long I've been using it, a bit about what is on it and why I visit it so often.

The website is the BBC news website. You can find it at http://www.bbc.co.uk/news but I just have it as a favorite on my toolbar. I am a complete BBC junkie. I visit the website several times a day if I can, and have been using it for as long as I can remember. Possibly for as long as the website has been in existence but definitely for the past ten years or more.

The BBC news website is massive. It contains rolling headlines of breaking news, and from the landing page you can jump to sections on different types of news categories. For example there are tabs for world news, health issues, environmental reports, sport, education and science as well as entertainment and arts stories. You can read just text based articles illustrated with a few pictures – which is my preferred way of accessing news and information – or you can opt to see news film or audio clips. I think the website is really comprehensive and easy to use too.

The BBC news website for me is a one-stop location for all current affairs and news items. I really like that I can see headlines of breaking news almost instantaneously, but it also includes more thoughtful reporting detailed online articles with considered analysis about global or local events. I can also find out what the weather forecast is – always handy in the UK where it can change so quickly, plus I like to be able to keep an eye on what is happening locally to me in Sheffield where I live. I also trust the BBC website to give balanced reporting. I think it has journalistic integrity, so I feel if I read it every day, I will have a good perspective on what is going on in the world, and enough information to come to my own conclusions on current affairs across the globe. The only downside of the website is that I find it can be a bit addictive! Because it is updated frequently it is tempting to keep going back and having another look if there is some running news item that I am following. It can lead me to procrastinate when I am supposed to be working, but I tell myself it is important to keep up to date with what is going on in the world, even though I know that really, it wouldn't hurt to limit myself to a news 'fix' just a couple of times a day.

I wonder if you use the website too, and if you do, whether you might as avid a follower as me.

Sample Answer 2:

I've been using the internet for more than 10 years and from the very beginning till now there are some websites those I use almost every day. www.yahoo.com is one of those web-sites and possibly I'll use this site forever. www.yahoo.com is basically an e-mail service provider and a very popular search engine. I can still remember my first day at a cyber-cafe where I opened the first web site of my life and that was yahoo.com and the cafe owner helped me to open an e-mail address and I still use this email address to send and receive e-mails and for chatting. www.yahoo.com is a popular search engine possibly next to www.google.com but as an e-mail service provider it is more popular than www.google.com in my country .This web-site has many other useful features like the homepage contains up-to-date news and feeds. It also gives the option to open free websites to its users etc. www.my.yahoo.com is a very popular service and recently the www.answers.yahoo.com has become one of the most popular questions and answers web-site that's millions of people are using.

Sample Answer 3:

I use internet daily and there are lots of websites that I often browse for different reasons. But probably www.facebook.com is the one I most often browse. It is a social networking website and probably is one of the top 5 most visited websites in the world. The website mainly facilitates me stay connected with my friends and helps me update and broadcast my news as well.

Though the primary purpose of this website is to let people communicate friends and known people but there are lots of other features as well. It offers games, ecommerce facility, emailing, chatting, making new friends, social marketing, different campaign, fan page opening etc. I have been using the website from 2004 and it is important to me because all of my friends and relatives are connected there. If a friend has a birthday, the website notifies me and I can wish him/ her a birthday, if someone has a new photo or news to share, I can see it from my account. I can share my photo, video, updates, thought as well. If someone opines on an issue, others can comment on it. For me, the website is important because my childhood friends, adolescence friends, college & University friends are connected there. I get their updates regularly and can let them know what's happening over here. In no other way I could have been connected to the people I am now connected via Facebook. I use this website from my computer and from my cell phone as well. For me this is a social networking website where I remain close to my friends and relatives. But with its own right it has become a powerful ecommerce platform, gaming place, marketing channel, and many more other business related platform.

Nowadays everybody owns a Facebook ID. Making new friends is easy in Facebook and that helps people grow their friends beyond boundary. Millions of people use Facebook and it is almost impossible to connect with people you care and know without this website.

Sample Cue Card 10

Describe a journey you went on.

You should say:
- ➤ Where you went
- ➤ Why you went to this particular place
- ➤ What you did and with whom

And describe why you enjoyed your journey/if not why.

Sample Answer 1:

I like visiting famous places and whenever I get vacation, I try to visit new places or places that I have heard about. One such trip that I took with one of my friends was a journey to Holland. I would like to talk about this tour to Holland that we took 2 years age.

Both of us (*me and my friend*) wanted to visit Holland and specifically Amsterdam, Hague and Rotterdam very much because we saw pictures and heard stories from friends about how beautiful and wonderful the place is. So finally we applied for visa, bought plane tickets, booked a hotel, packed our bags and our trip began.

We spent a lot of time before our holiday, researching of all the interesting places to visit and all the sights to see. So we went to Rijks museum, Van Gogh museum, Amstell Beer museum, took a romantic sunset cruise in the water channels, drove to Volendam, a small prettiest fisherman village, visited a cheese farm. We went to Rotterdam, which is the architecture city of Holland that stimulates innovation. We enjoyed the architectures and building there as much as we did walking in the neat roads and besides the beaches. Visiting the famous Anne Frank house was an exciting moment for me. I've read the Anne Frank's Diary in my early childhood and witnessing the place was very much exciting.

Every evening we took long walks along the channels, resting in small gardens, which Amsterdam has a lot of. Street artists were performing everywhere and a lot of people came to watch their show.

We enjoyed very much everything we did and especially in such a beautiful country. Having my friend by my side on this trip made it even more fun. Since we have never been to Holland, everything we saw and did seemed interesting and completely new to us. The people, their way to interpretation their culture attracted us very much. Before leaving the place, both of us agreed that the place is worth visiting and someday we would come back to re-explore it.

Sample Answer 2:

Once I was reading an article when I came across the lines of Rabindranath Tagore highlighting the beauty of Taj Mahal. It stated, "*The Taj Mahal rises above the banks of the river like a solitary tear suspended on the cheek of time.*" The lines encouraged me to visit the monument of love, The Taj Mahal.

Taj Mahal is included in the Seven Wonders of the World. So, before even I think of visiting any other site, it becomes more of a responsibility to give a visit to the heritage site of India. It was the prime reason I visited Taj Mahal.

It was a short trip with my family. My parents and my brother accompanied on my trip. It was a fun-filled trip as after a long time I got an opportunity to spend time with my family. Moreover, we opted for a road trip so that we had the flexibility to visit other famous places in Agra. It is rightly said, that journey matters, and not the destination, and this is what I experienced during my short-trip.

Sample Cue Card 11

> # Describe someone in your family who you really admire.
>
> **You should say:**
> - ➢ What relation this person is to you
> - ➢ What are your first memories of this person
> - ➢ How often you see this person
>
> **And explain why you really admire this person.**

Sample Answer 1:

I've got a small family with only five members and all of us are very close to each other and we love each other very much. Among them, I love my mother more than anyone else in the whole world. I adore my mother for her caring, loving, adorable behaviors and wit. She is the person I can share everything with and that's the reason I worship her so much.

Possibly she was the first human I saw when I opened my eyes in this world. A relationship with a mother is divine and all of my childhood memories are either related to my mom or my school. I can still remember a day I was late to come back home after school and that's because there was a ceremony at the school I did not know about. All of a certain I found that my mother was entering through the school gate to find me. I was so frightened that my mother would rebuke me for being late unnoticed and she must be mad at me. But to my best surprise, when my mother saw me she had a warm smile on her face that I'll never forget till my last breath on this earth. Then she hugged me and gave me a kiss. I felt then that I love my mother more than me. She attended the program at the school and afterwards we came back home together.

I spent my 19 years or so with my father and mother but I stay at a metropolitan city now for my education. Whenever I get a vacation, I meet my mother at my village home. On an average, I spend 2/3 months with my mother each year but I talk to her over the phone almost twice a day.

The reasons why I admire her are endless. She is caring, tender, she has got a big heart and she possesses a great love for everyone. She had been an ideal mother to raise 3 kids and making sure our education and moral values. She had made a lot of sacrifices all of her life and had never complained about anything to my best knowledge. She is the person who reminds me the power of love and caring.

Sample Answer 2:

A person I admire is my "*Mother*" because she is a fighter. You may ask why? To start, my mom got pregnant with me at the age of 18 and she did not have the support of my grandparents. Her own parents wanted to kick her out the house when they found out. She convinced them to let her stay, but she could not ask them for any help when raising the baby. Knowing all this my mom still decided to have the baby.

Besides not having the support of her parents, she also did not receive any help from my father. Although my father cared about me, he never gave my mom money or clothes to help her maintain me as a baby. She had to provide for me on her own. Going to school and working was killing her, but she wanted me to have a good life so she did anything that she could. My mom got pregnant again two years later, with the same man. The only thing was this time - it was worse. He left her life completely and her dad was sick. Therefore, he could no longer work. Now, not only did she have to provide for her two babies, but also for her parents. She was overwhelmed with everything happening. She didn't know what to do.

Finally, she decided to attend college and become a teacher for she can support the family she was now in charge of. It was not an easy thing to do. After she finished college it took her a while to find a job. It is not easy to find a job in Nicaragua. However, my mom never quit, no matter how hard things got for her she fought through it. To provide for her kids and parents.

Sample Answer 3:

I have got 6 family members and all of them are very dear and close to me. If I need to pick one family member among them to talk about, that would be my father. My father's name is (*say your father's name*) and he is around 55 years old. He is the kind of person I would want my offspring to be. He did his graduation in a time when formal education was not people's first choice. They would rather start earning from work rather than going to school. My father fought to ensure his education with the people who thought working or doing some sort of business has more value than education. But my father believed that education is the most important part of a man's life. He heartily held the idea that education shapes a man's life and is the kind of power and asset that would always accompany him.

I have lots of memories of my father and I see him every day. There exists a strong bonding between us that only two of us feel. I still remember those days of my childhood when I used to wait in the evening for my father to return from office. He would then play with me and help on completing my lessons. I vividly remember him sometimes taking me to the market and buy me gifts. When I was an infant he moved to the city from the village to ensure me better schooling and environment. That was a decision that has changed my life path. He himself helped me finishing my home works and lessons, always allured me of gifts if I could complete my study. Besides my education, he taught me lots of moral values and important things of life.

He used to work in a Government organization and for his hard-working and kindness. He is revered by all of our relatives, his friends and neighbors.

He believes in humanity, good behavior, our creator, and leads a life that can be exemplary. He still does most of his own works and helps my mom on her household works. After retirement, he has picked 2 new habits. Gardening and teaching neighbors' kids. He is a quiet and intelligent man who has benevolent heart and that what make him so admirable to me. He is still the pillar of our family and all of our family members love and respect him very much.

Sample Cue Card 12

Describe a person who accidentally became your friend.

You should say:
- ➢ Who the person is
- ➢ How you met him/her
- ➢ What made you two become friends

And explain how your friendship is now.

Sample Answer:

Though I have many friends, my friendship with them grew up with times and mutual understanding. But I can recall that my friendship with George grew up almost all of a sudden.

George is senior to me by 2 years and I did not meet him until I was in the 3rd semester in my University. One of my term final exam's schedules was changed and I did not know that. According to my previous exam schedule, I reached my University and was totally confused what to do when I heard that the exam was already over. I went to our Departmental head's office and he could not find a way around of it. He blamed me that I should have been more careful about the changes. I explained to him that I was sick and did not come to the University for 3-4 days and that made me unaware of the exam schedule changes. Then I found that someone who was sitting next to me in the departmental head's office asked me to meet the course teacher and explain the situation. He then escorted me to our course teacher's room and talked to the teacher. It seemed to me that George was already personally known to our teacher and they had an intimate relationship. Hearing everything the teacher agreed to arrange an exam for me next day in his office room.

My friendship with George grew up after that event and albeit our age difference, we found that we had many common interests and habits. We started spending time and I visited his home many times. We worked in a retail shop for about 8 months and that helped us become more intimate.

George is now staying in the USA and we do not meet each other in person. But we have online communications and we often let each other know our updates.

Sample Cue Card 13

Describe a friend from your childhood.

You should say:
- ➢ How you met him/her
- ➢ How long you are friends & what you did together
- ➢ What made you like him/ her

And explain your friendship.

Sample Answer 1:

I am going to tell you about my first '*best friend*' from childhood. I'll explain how we met, how long we were friends, what we got up to and why I liked her so much, and I'll try and explain our friendship so you can understand why we were so close.

I first met my friend Tracey when I went to junior school. We were sat next to each other in class, I don't think we chose to do that particularly, we probably just sat where we were told to on our first day of the school year, but we got on straight away and were firm friends from the age of about 8 until we left school to go to senior school aged about eleven. We happened to go to different schools at that point, and sadly our friendship drifted apart, when we were younger though, we were inseparable.

Tracey and I had similar interests. We liked being outside, we liked horses (*although neither of us went riding or had access to ponies back then*), we enjoyed doing craft type activities (*although she was really talented creating amazing pictures and artwork, whilst I just got stuck at the stage of coloring in*). My main memory is of us heading off together on our bikes for hours and hours at a time. She lived quite near a large park, so I used to cycle to her house, and then we'd go to the park together with a picnic lunch and spend all day playing games together. I'm embarrassed now to think how we galloped around pretending to be horses or whatever the game of the day was, but it was fun at the time. We used to try hula hooping and skipping too, seeing who could hold up a hoop for the longest of skip without stopping using a rope. I have a feeling she was more accomplished than me at both these activities too. Sometimes we would try to find and catch grasshoppers (*we always let them go*) or we would just laze in the sun until it was time to go home. It was very different then. There were no mobile phones, and people were much more relaxed about letting their children go off and play all day, I'm not sure if you could still do that. Still, we were very happy, and used to come back to her house tired and hot and sunburnt, and if we were lucky her mum would give us lemonade to drink and sometimes cheese salad rolls for tea. Happy memories indeed.

In terms of why we liked each other, well we just did. We enjoyed doing the same things. We could talk about anything to each other – complaining about school work or annoying parents and other such troublesome worries of the time. She had pet rabbits, and I had pet guinea pigs, so looking after our pets was a shared interest too. It probably helped that we lived quite close to each other and both had bikes too. We also both had a vivid imagination. It meant we could have remarkable adventures together pretending to inhabit whole new worlds that we had invented for ourselves.

We kept in touch for a while, but both eventually moved on. I think she went on to become an artist of some renown, which was not surprising given her early talent for art. Whatever she does and wherever she ended up I hope she is happy and successful too, and I will always remember her as a brilliant companion from when I was young, I wonder if she remembers me too.

Sample Answer 2:

Childhood has its specialty and magic and sometimes childhood friends are unforgettable. One such friend I recall was Steve who I still remember. Our friendship lasted only for a year and after that, he moved to a different city with his parents. I met him at our first day in school. I was late for school due to a bad traffic and when I reached my classroom, I thought that all of the seats have been occupied and I was desperately looking for a place to sit. The class teacher asked my name and announced to make a seat for me. I found that one of the boys was asking me to go over there and sit beside him. This very boy was Steve and I was grateful to him.

In the tiffin time, I shared my foods with him and talked about lots of things. From that next day, we started sitting next to each other and our friendship began to flourish. I found that he collects stamps as a hobby and I was excited to find this common hobby between us. We were very close friends and after one year I heard that he would be moving to a new city as his father has been transferred there. I did not know his postal address and as a consequence, I could not communicate him. We did not meet each other after that but he was such a good and close friend that I still miss him sometimes.

We did a lot of interesting and fun stuff together. At school, we played footballs and other games in the interval period. We made kites and flew them together, we went to many places to buy stamps, we went to the library to read books, we went to the river to swim, we climbed in trees, we played crickets, we walked in the streets and told stories to each other and did many other things together.

He was a lively and helpful boy who liked me very much. We had many things in common and we helped each other on our studies. Since I enjoyed participating different activities with him, I liked him as a friend as well. We had a strong bonding and intimate friendship between us. We tried to help each other whenever needed.

Sample Cue Card 14

> # Describe a hotel you have stayed in.
>
> **You should say:**
> - Where the hotel is
> - Why you stayed at that particular hotel
> - Give details description of the hotel and the view from it
>
> **And explain what makes the hotel special.**

Sample Answer 1:

Is it cheating if I tell you about a Bed and Breakfast I stayed in rather than a hotel? I'm going to risk it, and tell you all about a place I stayed on holiday, what it was like and why it was so special to me.

Many years ago I lost my job. I'd been covering a post while someone was on maternity leave, but then they came back and I found I didn't have a job. Anymore! To cheer me up, two good friends of mine suggested we went away for a weekend break. One of them had found a really nice Bed and Breakfast in Anglesey, which is an Island off the coast of Wales. Nowadays it doesn't feel so much like an island anymore because it is permanently attached to the mainland by the very famous 'Menai Bridge'. She chose the place partly because of its spectacular location – it is surrounded by sea - but also because it was vegetarian (*we all were too*) and offered horse riding, which was a hobby, we had in common.

The B&B as we call them in the UK, was, well, pretty eccentric. It was a lovely old house, with quirky rooms, dubious cleanliness and an assortment of dogs, cats, hens, ducks, ponies, and people – pretty chaotic. From the house, you could see across the Menai Straits, the stretch of sea between Anglesey and the mainland, to the snow-topped mountains of Snowdonia. It was glorious. The proprietor was one of those people who very much spoke her mind, but took you as you were, she quickly involved us in life on her small holding, feeding animals, heading off to the beach and drunkenly putting the world to rights in front of an open fire in the evening. We walked the dogs, fed the hens and galloped the horses along deserted beaches.

When the woman who owned the B&B found I didn't have a job, she said quite simply *'well, why don't you come and work for me?'* I was flabbergasted, I'd never really considered that sort of a job, and I'd come on holiday not looking for employment. I hesitated, but she persisted. *'If you like it you can stay, if you don't you can leave – where is the risk in that?'* To cut a long story short, with unusual spontaneity and recklessness I agreed. For the next two years, I worked at the B&B looking after the horses and guests, taking out rides along the beautiful Welsh beaches and enjoying a rural lifestyle. It was brilliant, I learned a lot about animals, people and myself, and had many adventures along the way. I didn't earn much, but I lived well in a caravan in the middle of a field with hens clucking around outside and ponies scratching their bottoms on the door of my accommodation in the mornings.

So for me, that remote Anglesey B&B will always be very special, because it introduced me to a different way of living and working, and gave me an appreciation of the countryside that I hadn't really been able to experience before. I don't think I've ever laughed as much doing a job as I did staying there.

Sample Answer 2:

The hotel that I stayed in 2 years back while my visit to India, is Westin. I had an official tour to Pune, India and my office arranged the stay in Westin. The reason I stayed in this particular hotel is mostly because my office arranged our stay there. But that was a really great experience. Since Westin is a renowned hotel chain and I have experienced their superb service in our country, I was excited to be in Westin in Pune as well.

The hotel has been placed in a distinctive location in the beautiful Koregaon Park along the Mula Mutha River and is just five kilometers from the airport. Westin is also in the vicinity is Magarpatta and Hadapsar, an information technology hotspot. Industrial parks lie within a 25-kilometer radius of this hotel. The staying rooms are subtly designed and give comfort to be there. The hotel includes club rooms, attractive and heavenly spa and workout gym, meeting room and exclusive restaurant. The rooms feature soft and comfortable bed and an eye-catching view overlooking green surroundings Mula Mutha River.

The Westin is a renowned hotel chain that offers exclusive customer experience. The view, the stay, the foods and facilities make the hotel a different experience.

Sample Cue Card 15

Describe what you usually do in your leisure time.

You should say:
- What you do
- Who you do it with
- Where you do it

And explain why you like to spend your free time this way.

Sample Answer:

I have classes 5 days in a week, I attend a diploma course on Computing and I do some tuition as well and all of those activities and my study make my days busy. However, I maintain some leisure activities and in my day-off, I go through a different routine.

I love to read books and maintain my own blog. Whenever I get time either I read books or write/ moderate my blog. Besides reading and writing for my blog, I play some indoor games with my friends and family members like chess, computer games etc. If it's an outdoor game, I play with my neighbors or friends.

I read book mostly in my study room and sometimes in the nearby library. I work on my computer to update my blogs. I mostly read fictions and historical books. The blog I maintain is mostly technology related and I add the details with images for my blog readers. Two friends of mine are now the moderator of this blog and they contribute to this blog as well.

I like to utilize my leisure time and enjoy very much what I do. Reading book is the most prudent investment of leisure time and I learn many things from reading. Maintaining a blog is a great way improving the writing and sharing knowledge and that helps me greatly to explore new things as I need to read a lot to generate ideas to write.

The indoor game like chess is a great way of passing time and also helps doing some brainstorming. I take part in the outdoor games to both enjoy the game and to keep my body and mind fresh and fit.

Sample Cue Card 16

Describe an important decision/ choice that you made in your life.

You should say:
- ➢ What the decision was
- ➢ When you took the decision
- ➢ What are the results of the decision was and whether it was a good choice

And explain why it was an important decision or choice for you.

Sample Answer 1:

Actually I'm not always good at making decisions. I worry about making wrong choices, and often seek advice from friends to help me think through the consequences of picking one option over another. Mind you, some people say that we choose who to ask for advice depending on what advice we want to hear. That might be true. Some decisions are easy to make – perhaps because all the possible options are good ones (*like choosing a favorite pudding*) others seem to have no good options only '*least bad*' ones, those are hardest to make. The important decision I can think of, and which I'm going to talk about today, worked out in the end, but it was terrifying to have to make at the time.

I'll talk you through what the decision was, when I took it and what the results were. Finally, I'll explain why it was so important that it still impacts on me today.

The decision was whether or not I should relocate to a different part of the country to take up a new job. I had to make the decision about 6 years ago. I had been self-employed for a while, but then there was a downturn in the economy and I stopped getting enough work to support myself. I applied for a job in Sheffield, which was a city I didn't know at all, and when I had first an interview, and then a job offer, I was faced with a big decision. Should I leave my home and friends to start a new life in Sheffield for a promising job at a prestigious university; or should I stay where I was in my lovely house and familiar surroundings, and hope the work might pick up again in the future.

I thought a lot about the pros and cons; I cried a lot to be honest, as the thought of making a new start was really scary. I'd be all on my own, and what if I didn't make friends or couldn't do the job well? However, ultimately it came down to income. I couldn't live on fresh air, and this was a well-paid job. I also thought if I turned the work down, and then didn't manage to pick up new contracts I'd always wonder '*what if?*' or how might things have been different if I'd just been brave enough to '*give it a go*' I accepted the job and started to pack. In less than three weeks I was renting a flat in a new city and turning up to work in a new office with new colleagues. One resolution I made early on, was to be really positive about the decision once I'd made it. I'd join societies, say '*yes*' to every social invitation, and really try to build a new life quickly. I wouldn't ever look back!

The result of the decision, Well, I moved to a new city, and took a new job. It was hard at first, there was a lot to learn and sometimes it was lonely too. However, I've never regretted it. Sheffield is a lovely city near to beautiful countryside. I've rented an attic flat which has great views over the city in one direction and woodland in the other. I think this city must be one of the friendliest ones in the UK, people were incredibly welcoming to me as a newcomer, and there are always lots to do. I don't have that job anymore, but I don't regret taking it at all. I do sometimes miss my old house in Leamington where I used to live, but I don't miss anything else. I think the move revitalized me and took me on a great new adventure, sometimes you do just have to take a bit of a risk in life to progress, this bit of risk taking worked for me.

So in conclusion, I think it was a big decision, but I made a good choice. Of course, it was an important one as it changed everything for me, from where I lived and worked, to who my friends are. Honestly though, I think perhaps with decisions it matters less what you decide, and more that once you have made a decision you make the best of it, wherever it may take you. Sometimes the journey is speedy and smooth, sometimes it is rocky along the way, but whatever path we choose, it is what makes us the people we are – for better or worse.

Sample Answer 2:

I've made lots of decisions in my life and frankly I have taken those decisions sometimes all alone and sometimes discussing with my parents and others. The particular decision that seems very important to me was the time when I decided to major in Literature rather than major in Engineering. My mother wanted me to get admitted in the Eng. University and do my graduation majoring Engineering while my fascination was studying in Literature. I made this decision when I was 18 years of old, just after finishing my 12th grade. My father did not force me to do anything; instead, he told me to do what I thought was best for me. My relatives thought that I was a fool and too immature to make a big decision for myself.

But after considering several issues and perspective I decided to get myself admitted in a University that offers graduation in Literature. I'm happy that I made this decision. I'm yet to finish my graduation but throughout the last 3 years I have enjoyed studying literature and I am doing quite well academically.

Making the decision/ choice was not easy and I had to go through a hard time as I remember. I had to fight a lot with my inner self and then convince my mother. There were always risks of picking the option I prefer my parents would have complained if I hadn't made a promising result. I still remember the dubious feelings I had that time. Sometimes it seemed to me that I should abandon my passion and yield to my parents' decision and then again I strongly felt for my own choice and passion. Since I made my own choice at that time, a strong urge and force worked on me that I have to do really good and I am happy that I took my decision and doing very good so far.

Sample Cue Card 17

Describe something special you want to buy in the future.

You should say:
  ➢ What it is
  ➢ What it is like
  ➢ When you intend to buy it
And explain why you want to buy it.

Sample Answer 1:

So, I've been asked to talk about 'something special that I'd like to buy in the future, it's quite tricky to know how to respond to this topic. Should I pick something that I'd love to buy, but isn't realistic (*like a rainbow*). Something that I'd love to buy as a gift for someone else (*treat my mum to afternoon tea at a posh hotel*) or something practical for me (*I could really do with a new pair of winter shoes*). In fact, I'm going to go with the first thing that popped into my head when you told me the theme – I'm going to talk about something that I would really like to buy, but haven't quite got around to yet.

I'm going to tell you what it is, what is like, when I intend to buy it and why it is I'd like this particular item so much.

The special thing I have in mind is a photo book. You can get them on the internet I think. You select a range of digital photos that are special or meaningful to you, and then arrange them electronically with captions and dates and so on. Then there are specialist companies that will put them together in a traditionally bound physical book.

The idea is quite a simple one, but genius. In this age of digital cameras it's easy to take lots and lots of photographs, some are good, some are funny, and some are indifferent. Many are bizarre; others are hilarious; and some are just terrible, but all of them are quite literally snapshots of memories. However, because now photographs are everywhere, I think we take them a bit for granted and don't appreciate them as much as we should. The really great photographs get lost in the multitude of average or terrible ones. There are so many files of photos on my computer, that I can't even remember what they contain, let alone where the most important ones are stored anymore. So what I'd love to do is take the time to pick out a selection that are really important to me, and have them brought together in an album that I can treasure and look back on, and share with others. Honestly, nobody really wants to look at 1000 pictures of your holiday/ family/ pet, but they might like to look at half a dozen of each that had been carefully chosen to tell a particular story, and it's fun to share such memories.

When do I intend to do this? Well, interestingly, I have a 'to do' list on my desk. One of the items that have been on it for some years is 'sort through my photos'. I never get around to it. Maybe now I've been made to reflect on it, I should prioritize this task. Just because it has never felt urgent (*that is, something I need to do immediately*) this activity never makes it to the top of my list. However, it is important. I need to make time for it. Maybe next week – I should give myself a deadline.

I hope you can see already why I'd like to buy this so much. But if I need to explain more, it is because I think by making a selection of really important pictures, I can pick out special memories. By putting these together in a physical book I think they will endure longer and be valued more than if they are lost in the millions and millions of images that fill the internet. Even today, I have on my shelves books that are over a hundred years old, they have pages that have slightly yellowed with age, but are perfectly useable and readable. On the other hand I have a pile of floppy discs, I have no idea what is on them anymore, and I no longer have a computer that I could read them on, effectively, those contents are lost forever. Despite how clever we are in this digital age, I have a suspicion that it is our books that will outlast us all, not pixels in cyberspace. What do you think?

Sample Answer 2:

I have a personal list (*wish list you can say*) that has many things that I want to buy in future. One such special thing that I want to buy in near future is a personal car. I mostly use public transportation to move from one place to another and to visit my hometown which is very inconvenient. Owning a car would be a great advantage for me as I would be able to freely move and visit my home town more frequently.

The car I want to buy is the Fusion Hybrid car by Ford. This is a stylish looking car which is also fuel efficient. My preference would be white color. I intend to buy it after 2-3 years as it would allow me to save the money and apply for the car loan I need to purchase it.

There are so many advantages of owning a car especially in the city I live in. Maintaining the perfect timing is pretty tough if you travel in a public bus. You would need to wait for the bus, stay in the long queue for a long. And the frequency of the public buses and the number of people do not allow one to maintain the timing one needs to keep. If I own my own car I'd be able to avoid the usual bad traffic and take the alternatives roads. Travelling in a public bus is inconvenient and you do not have any privacy in it. With my own car I'd be able to go to my hometown and visit my parents more frequently than I do now.

Sample Answer 3:

I know exactly what the special thing is that I want to buy in the future. In fact, I'd like to buy it right now, as soon as I've finished talking to you today. I'm going to tell you what it is, what it is like, when I'll buy it and explain why it is I want to get it so urgently and so much.

The item is a spider catcher. Have you ever hear of them? They are a bit tricky to describe, but basically, it's a simple gadget that allows you to pick up a spider without hurting or touching it, so you can release it unharmed elsewhere. There are different designs, but the one I like the look of has a long handle with a trigger mechanism at one end which operates some soft gentle bristles at the other. If you believe the adverts, it works by surrounding the spider with bristles that close around it, forming a harmless trap, which allows you to pick up and release the spider without squashing it. To operate it you simply squeeze the lever to open the bristles, position the open bristles over the spider, and then release the lever so they gently close around it. You can then pick up the spider and release it somewhere else – a long way away - by once again squeezing the lever to reopen the trap. Apparently it doesn't harm the creature, it also promises *'no mess, safe and easy to use'*.

So that's what it is called and how it is supposed to work. I'd like to buy it soon. Why? Because I have a completely irrational fear of spiders! It is very specific though, I don't think I have true arachnophobia, I'm fine with even very large spiders if they are outside, but there is a certain form of house spider we have here in the UK which always makes me jump. They are quite large, they can grow to about 12 – 14 centimeters in size, and the males become active in houses around autumn (October time). At this time of year they leave their webs in search of a female, and will move inside to the drier environment of a house after a summer living outside or in sheds. They prowl about looking for female mates. They move very erratically, and quite high up on their legs, plus they have a tendency to loiter in corners or shoot across the floor, where if the light hits them they cast a ridiculously disproportionate shadow. They can't hurt you, and they are only looking for love, but my how they frighten me if I just catch sight of one unexpectedly. The reason I want to buy a spider catcher soon, is that I have just this morning seen an ENORMOUS spider prowling about my living room. I really don't like sharing my flat with him, even though he means me no harm. Once you have seen one spider there will be more, the next few weeks will bring many such monster spiders into my home, and I want to be prepared.

Catching these spiders is hard. One method I use is to put a glass or jug over the spider, and then slide a piece of paper underneath so you can trap the spider and let it go outside. The problem with this method though is that sometimes the spiders are too big to fit under a glass. Also, they move so fast, they can be gone before you get a chance to catch them, and finally, I don't really like getting so close to them in the attempt to get them. The spider catcher seems like the perfect solution. I wouldn't want to harm the spider, it isn't its fault I'm scared, but I'd prefer not to have them running around all over the place either! That's why I really, really want a spider catcher of my own. It sounds like the perfect solution for fearful me, facing a potential parade of spiders stomping about when I'm all alone watching a horror film on TV at night as autumn draws in.

Sample Cue Card 18

Describe a happy event of your life.

You should talk about:
- ➢ What the event was
- ➢ When it occurred
- ➢ Why it was a memorable and happy event for you

And give any details of the event.

Sample Answer:

There are numerous happy events in my life that I can recall and among them I would like to talk about the day that I was blessed with a little sister. This was an event that I still recall vividly. I was then only 7-8 years old and when I saw a little angel was crying on my mother's lap, I became the happiest man in the world. I was the only son of my parents and when I heard that I will have another sibling, I got very excited and I was counting days when this brother/ sister of mine will come. I speculated and imagined lots of things I would do with my sibling. The day that my sister came in to the world was one of the happiest days of my life.

For the first time I felt a strong urge to kiss this little fairy child. She was so beautiful and adorable that I thanked God for the gift. My mother asked me to hold her and kiss her but I was afraid to touch her as I thought that might hurt her. I felt like I was flying on that day. My mother gave birth of the baby in a hospital and I was so happy and attached by the event that I denied returning home at night. I stayed in the hospital cabin for about 4-5 days till my mother and sister came home. I came back home with the most precious gift of the world.

Sample Cue Card 19

> ## Describe a positive change in your life.
>
> **You should say:**
> - ➤ What the change was about
> - ➤ When it happened
> - ➤ Describe details of the change happened
>
> **And describe how it affected you later life.**

Sample Answer 1:

You have asked me to think back on some change I've made in my life, that turned out to be one for the better. I am going to tell you what the change was and when it happened. I'll give you a bit of detail about how things were different for me after the change and finish by describing what it means for me now, a bit later in life. The funny thing about changes is that you don't always recognize them at the time. For me, I didn't know when I started out that the positive change I was making would turn out to be a long term difference in my behavior. However, it turned out to be just that. It is only looking back now that I can identify there was a definite shift in what I got up to, and I can even pinpoint a definite time, but in the midst of it all I had no idea where that change would take me.

The change was basically that I decided I needed to get a bit fitter, and the thing that helped me do so was joining up to do Parkrun. However, I'm jumping ahead. Let me explain how it came about. A couple of years ago I started to feel like I was getting old and losing my basic fitness. Although I walked quite a lot (*as a form of transport, as well as to enjoy the local countryside*) I wasn't really doing anything else very much that was physical. I was never very good at sports, so I didn't really know where to begin. However, I've always liked being outdoors, so on something of a whim I booked an activity holiday in Northumberland, which is a beautiful rural area in the north east of England, right by the coast. The holiday was great. We did abseiling; hill walking; body-surfing – all sorts of things. In addition, every morning began with a run along the sands of the seaside. Now I'd never run before – well only if I was trying to catch a bus, but otherwise, not at all. I wasn't very good at it, and honestly, I didn't even really enjoy it all that much. However, I did have to concede that it is a great form of exercise. You don't really need any special equipment (*apart from decent trainers*). You can do it anywhere and it's free. What's more, I found out from some other holiday makers that in the UK there is a free weekly event held nationwide in parks all over the country. It is called Parkrun, and basically people gather every Saturday morning at 9.00 a.m. to run a fixed course of 5km and get a time for doing so. I wasn't too sure if this would be achievable for me. I'd never run that far before. But I promised myself I would try it '*just once*' to see if I could.

The day after I got back from my holiday I turned up to do the Parkrun at my local park. I can tell you the exact day. It was 25th September 2015. I know this, because the whole point of Parkrun is that if you register (*which is free*) then the organization records your time each week and you can access it on line afterwards. The first time I went I didn't even manage to run the whole way round, but I did finish, and I did get a great sense of achievement. Because you know your time, it is quite addictive, you find you do want to go again the next week and see if you can improve. My local parkrun is huge, with well over 500 runners taking part every week – so even though I was pretty slow, I found I wasn't the slowest.

Since that day over two years ago, I've found that I've gone to Parkrun almost every week. I have taken part in some 70 parkruns, and through doing so made new friends, maintained a certain level of fitness, and even gained the confidence to take part in some longer runs. I've done lots of 10km races now, a few off-road runs – including one over 24km as well as taken part in obstacle races! I would never have believed that the small change of '*just going once*' to Parkrun to '*give it a go*' would lead to me being such an enthusiastic member of Parkrun two years later. By the way, I haven't really ever got any faster, but I'm definitely a lot fitter. Now I can't imagine a Saturday morning without heading off for a run with my 500 friends at the local park. That first day I turned up nervously to join in with Parkrun was definitely the beginning of a positive change in my life.

Sample Answer 2:

The positive change that I would like to talk about is '*I started playing outdoor games instead of playing computer games*'. After I got my first personal computer when I was only

9 years old or so, I started learning many things. Besides that I started playing the computer games. As computer games are addictive I found that I was playing the games whenever I had spare times. This addiction barred me from playing outdoor games like cricket, football etc.

I found myself very much attracted to the computer games and I preferred to play the games at home instead of going to open spaces or fields to participate in outdoor games that involve physical exercises. Not that computer games are all so bad, but playing them all the time someone has got is not a good thing especially for kids. I found that I was spending more times at home than being outside. After my parents noticed that, they discussed with me about that and explained me the importance of outdoor activities. They gave me strict restriction that I would only be able to play computer games for an hour daily and in the evening I'd have to go outside to play with my friends.

This was obviously a very positive change for me. I'm not against computer games but I feel that if there are more important things to do, then we should not spend time on computer games only.

This change affected me very positively. I became a good cricket player later on, I started maintaining my times more prudently and I am sure this change has affected me positively in terms of physical and mental health.

Sample Cue Card 20

> ### Describe one of your favorite photographs.
>
> **You should say:**
> - When the photograph was taken
> - What it looks like
> - What significant memory you have regarding this photograph
>
> **And explain why it is one of your favorite photographs.**

Sample Answer 1:

The photograph that was taken when I was only 4-5 years old with my parents, grandfather and grandmother is one of my very favorite photographs. I do not have clear memory regarding the event when the photograph was taken but I have seen it thousands times and still I look at it with a delight and sadness. The photograph is a black-and-white one and later I have enlarged it and framed it in my living room. The small kid (*me*), the grandparents and young parents make the picture a really significant one to me. I look with amazement in to the picture and sometimes can't believe I was so small and different looking at that time The picture gives me a gloomy feelings as my grandfather and mother are no longer with us. In the picture they look so lively but I can't be with them anymore.

I was wearing a full sleeve shirt, full pant and a pair of red shoes. In the picture I was in the middle and was sitting in a chair. Others were standing around me. My parents are on the right and my grandparents are on the left. My father was very stylish and was wearing fashionable dress in the picture. My grandfather had spectacles in his eyes and had his hair back-brushed. My mother and grandmother were wearing traditional dresses but both looked so fresh and happy in the picture.

This photograph is probably is my most favorite one ass it conveys my grandparents' memory and depicts a happy family. Every time I look at this particular picture, it gives a different sensation - mixture of happiness and sadness. This is a priceless possession to me and I would like to keep it with me for the rest of my life.

Sample Answer 2:

There was a time when photos were only taken by regular point-and-shoot-cameras, but now everything has changed. With the help of mobile phones and computers, people are taking billions of photos every day from all parts of the world. I, myself, take so many pictures that I sometimes forget which photograph I took and when I took it. There is this one photograph I like the most. It's just beautiful.

In this photograph I am carrying my niece and she is smiling up at me. I first saw the photograph about a week ago. I didn't even know the photograph existed until my sister showed it to me. I liked it so much that I made it the wallpaper background of my computer. Now, whenever I open the lip of my laptop, the first thing I see is that picture.

The photo shows happiness. I think it was taken four years ago, and shows how time has passed, how the world changes. After looking at the photograph, I remembered that my niece was crying a lot and my sister was about to give her to the nanny. At that moment I decided to step-in and hold her. Once I had her in my arms she got happy and smiled. At that perfect moment the photograph was taken. The picture shows a time when I was happy. It also shows at time when we all used to have an optimistic outlook of the world but now all optimism and love has just vanished from my life.

The photograph was taken when I was only 5 years old. I was with my parents and grandparents & it's one of my very favorite pictures ever. I do not have clear memory regarding the event when the photograph was taken but I have seen it a thousand times. To this day I still I look at it with delight and sadness. I had it enlarged and framed. It hangs in the living room where everyone can see the black and white. The small kid (*me*), the grandparents and young parents make the picture a really significant one to me. I look with amazement at the picture and sometimes I can't believe I was so small and different looking at that time. The picture gives me a sense of melancholy since my grandfather & grandmother is no longer with us. In the picture they seem so lively but I can't be with them anymore.

I was wearing a long sleeve shirt, pants and a pair of red shoes. In the picture I was in the middle, sitting on a chair. Others were standing around me. My parents are on the right and my grandparents are on the left. My father was very stylish and was dressed fashionably in the picture. My grandfather was wearing spectacles and had his hair back-brushed. My mother and grandmother were both wearing traditional dresses but both looked so fresh and happy in the picture.

This photograph is probably is my most favorite one as it conveys my grandparents' memory and depicts a happy family. Every time I look at this particular picture, I get the feeling of bitter sweetness! This is a priceless possession to me and I would like to keep it with me for the rest of my life.

Sample Cue Card 21

> # A famous person you know in your country.
>
> **You should say:**
> - Who the person is
> - Why is he famous
> - What makes you mention specifically him/ her
>
> **And describe what positive changes this person has brought for your country.**

Sample Answer 1:

I thought at first the cue card meant someone I know personally, or had actually met. That would be really hard. I'm not very well connected. There are so many famous people in my country – England, part of the United Kingdom. I could pick the Queen, I think she is one of the most recognized people the world over, but I think that's too easy and predictable. I'm going to pick instead a famous person from English history, you may never even have heard of her, but she is really important in terms of contributing to political change in my country, and although perhaps not everyone knows her name, most people would know about what she did.

I'll tell you who the person is, why she is famous and what makes me choose her. Finally, I'll try and explain how she has contributed to positive change in the UK.

This person is Emily Wilding Davison. She was born in the 1870s and died, famously, in June 1913. She is famous, or even infamous, because she was a militant activist who fought for women's suffrage – that is for women to have the same rights to vote as men - in Britain. She was one of a number of women who protested in different ways about the inequality that existed. At that time, only men were allowed to vote in elections, something that seems incredible today. Some of the protestors took direct action, leading to them being arrested and imprisoned for their views. Once imprisoned, some took it further and went on hunger strike, leading to them being force fed – Emily herself was jailed on numerous occasion nine I think, and force fed nearly fifty times. The reason though, that she is particularly remembered amongst the many women who campaigned so vociferously, is that it was her who apparently died for the cause. On 4th

June 1913, she stepped out in front of the King's own horse when it was racing as part of the famous race the Epsom Derby (*this horse race still takes place each year today*). She suffered fatal injuries, and died a few days later. There was a huge public funeral, and thousands of suffragettes accompanied the coffin and tens of thousands of people lined the streets of London.

People have different opinions about whether she actually intended to kill herself, or just to disrupt the race to bring attention to her cause. Personally, I think she would have wanted to live on to continue her protests and contribute to the debate, but her life was cut short aged only 40 years old, by accident. I have chosen her, because I think she was a brave and principled woman. I might not approve of all her actions, but without her efforts, and people like her, women would not have ultimately gained the vote in this country, which I consider to be a basic right. Women fought hard for that equality, so I think it's very important that all people (*men and women*) exercise their democratic right to vote. It was a right that was hard won but potentially easily lost. Democracy is an imperfect system, but it the political one we have in the UK, and I believe women and men should have equal influence in how it is executed. It takes courage sometimes, to stand up for what you believe in, and her courage cannot be disputed.

It is hard to say that any one action or person brought about the enfranchisement of women, but certainly her actions on that day brought the debate about women's equality to center stage. It led to more men supporting the campaign, widening the voices of arguing for equal rights and over time. Some women got the vote in 1918, after the first world war, but only those who were householders over the age of 30 (*6 million women*). Women over 21 did not get the vote until 1928, so perhaps it's only then you can say there was equality. She therefore contributed to the positive change of bringing about equal rights in voting for men and women in the UK.

Over time in this county, people have come to take the right to vote for granted, I think the contribution of the suffragettes in general and Emily Wilding Davison in particular might come to be forgotten over time. I was pleased therefore to hear that a new film is coming out on exactly this period of history, it's (*unsurprisingly*) called 'Suffragette'. I haven't seen it yet. I wonder how close it will be to the truth of those times – perhaps we'll never know.

Sample Answer 2:

I am from Australia and Hugh Jackman is one of the most famous persons in my country. His full name is Hugh Michael Jackman and he was born in 1968. He is a famous and critically acclaimed actor, producer and revered superstar for his superb performance in TV, film and musical theatre.

He is well known for the superhero character Wolverine in the X-Men series and his leading roles in many well-known movies like Australia, Kate & Leopold, Les Miserables, Van Helsing, The Prestige, Real Steel and Prisoners.

I mention specifically him because I'm a big fan of his acting and performance. I have seen almost all of his movies and TV serials and consider him to one of the world's most prominent actors alive.

He was born in Sydney, New South Wales, and graduated from University of Technology, Sydney, in 1991 with a BA in Communications. He is a philanthropist and is an active supporter for micro-credit. He is also one of the founders and the global advisor for the Global Poverty Project. Besides he is an ambassador of World Vision and participated in the climate week NYC ceremony. He is also an active supporter and donator for different charity and social welfare programs.

Through his acting, fame and donation he is trying to fight poverty and is trying to help the people in need. That's a great way of extending hand for people in need and can be exemplary for others.

He is a world renowned actor and is revered by his countrymen. Through his acting he has increased the impression of an Australian born actor and through his charity and philanthropic activity he is helping others.

> **Describe an important invention that you think has positively influenced human race.**
>
> **You should say:**
> - ➤ What the invention is
> - ➤ Who invented it
> - ➤ What changes it brought
>
> **And explain how it has positively influenced human race.**

Sample Answer:

It is really tough to pick one particular scientific invention that had positively influenced human race as there are possibly hundreds and thousands of such inventions. I would like to pick the '**Light Bulb**' as one such invention that has very positively influenced human race.

This single invention of science has uplifted the human race towards prosperity and modern world. Think about a world without any lights in the dark and we would have been no different than living in a cave. The great scientist Thomas Edison is credited to invent the light bulb and till then many improvements have been done to it.

The bulb is the main source of illumination and light at night time when the Sun is hiding in the opposite side of the world. We are so habituated with the electricity and light bulbs that we might wonder if it is a life changing invention or not.

But think about living your life for few days without the bulbs and then you would realize the true importance of this single invention. Some may argue that fuel powered lighting system could have been alternative to it, but the reality is that, that would have been too expensive and could not have been an easy source for lighting the houses,

Think about the other living beings other than human; they mostly get back to their living place in the evening and except some nocturnal animals and birds, most of them stay at their living place till the morning.

They rarely do anything at night and that's because they are afraid of dark and have no vision to see at night. As human, we could have some lighting system if we did not know how to light a bulb but that would not have been so widespread without the invention of light bulb. Scientific inventions are interrelated and one invention or theory inspired and accelerates the invention of other important inventions.

Light bulb is one such invention that has inspired the invention and research of other inventions. This is the single invention that has made us free from being active only at day time when the sun is there.

Sample Cue Card 23

> ## Describe a foreign country you have planned to visit.
>
> **You should say:**
> - Where the country is
> - When you are planning to visit there
> - Why you have planned to go there
>
> And give details of your planning to visit the country.

Sample Answer:

I have planned to visit Greece after my graduation is done. I have a relative there and he has invited me to visit his family several times. Earlier this year when I was promoted to the final year of my graduation, I have planned to visit at least one foreign country just after my graduation day. I have considered many countries and finally planned to visit Greece. It is a country in southern Europe and has around 11 million populations.

I have planned to visit Greece in the middle of the next year and would stay there for about one month. The relative I have there is my maternal uncle and he lives at Athens with his family. There is a good chance that I will be staying with them during my visit there. Greece is a culturally rich country that offers the visitors and tourists a lot of amazing activities, splendid sceneries, museums, diverse culture and many more. The museums, archaeological sites and the tours offer the chance to closely know the history of this country. The islands are the main characteristic of Greece's morphology and have become a big part of their custom and culture.

There are 2-3 main reasons I would like to visit the country. First, the invitation to visit my maternal uncle has been pending for several years and I thought it a good chance to meet them. Second, I am a big fan of mythology and Greek mythology was one of my most interesting readings for the last few years. Those stories have been so profoundly entertaining and thought provoking and suddenly I found a great desire to visit the place in person. Though things have changed there with time but the archaeological sites and museum would walk a visitor though the past and present and would amaze them.

This is an ideal place to stay and enjoy. This is a country of crossroad color of culture, history, diversity, warmth of friendliness, expectation, discover and expedition. For all those reasons I have decided to visit Greece in the next year.

Sample Cue Card 24

Describe a library that you visited.

You should say:
> ➤ Where it was
> ➤ What it looked like
> ➤ What facilities it had

And explain what influence it had on you and how you felt about it.

Sample Answer:

The library I'd like to talk about that I visited is 'Illumination Library' (*Tell the name of a library from your home town*) and it is situated in my home town. I have not visited this particular library for the last 2 years as I am not living in my hometown any longer and yet this is the library I will always remember. This library is situated at the center of our home town and occupies the whole 3 story building. There are plenty of books there and the library offers variety of books, novels, research papers, magazines and many more for people of different tastes.

The books are well catalogued and arranged in a convenient fashion. There are more than 3-4 librarians and several other assistants to help find any book. The library also offers membership facility and the active members are allowed to take books to home. Since the library is funded by government the membership fee is very negligible and affordable for students, there are lots of people visiting and reading there.

People of our hometown consider this library as the best place to gather knowledge, read in peace and to find reference books for study or professional reasons.

For me this library has a great influence on me. I became a member of this library when I was only 7 years old. My reading habit has been grown up from there. I became a passionate reader of books and novels and this library had a great influence on that. This library also helped me finishing some academic projects as I could find books and reference reading materials. I have read plenty of books in my childhood and adolescence time only because the library was conveniently there for me.

Sample Cue Card 25

> # Describe your holidays.
>
> **You should say:**
> - ➤ Where you go for the holidays
> - ➤ How long they last
> - ➤ Who you go with
>
> **And talk about anything interesting happens during your holidays.**

Sample Answer 1:

In most of my holidays I go to visit my family members in my hometown. For my job, I am currently residing in the capital city of my country but my parents, siblings, grandparents, uncle and aunts are living in our hometown. So in most of my holidays I go to visit my family members. My typical holidays last for 3-4 days most of the time and sometimes I get longer holidays.

When I was a university student, I had some friends studying in the same faculty who were from my hometown. During my university study we used to go to our hometown together on our vacations but now-a-days I go to my hometown mostly alone. The journey takes about 5-6 hours by bus. Sometimes we travel by train and this train journeys usually take 7-8 hours including the stoppage. Though the journey is tiresome sometimes, but the thought of meeting my family members and the excitement of being in the place I really love wash away the tiresomeness and monotonous feeling of the journey.

The time I stay with my family members and local friends, I enjoy the moments very much. This is the town where I grew up and naturally all of my childhood & adolescence memories are related to this place. I do lots of interesting things there during my holidays. I swim in the river, take care of the garden and firm we have, collect vegetables and fruits from our garden and then make arrangement to sell those to the local sellers, sometime I catch fished, play with my friends both indoor and outdoor games, visit different places and do lots of other stuffs.

In my city life, I have to follow a strict timeline and stay at office most of the time, but in my hometown where I mostly go during my holidays, I am quite free and do whatever I feel like doing and spend time with the people I care most. That's why I prefer to go to my hometown during my holidays rather than going to other places.

Sample Answer 2:

Thank you for the opportunity to talk about my holidays and I would like to talk it in details. I prefer to enjoy my holidays only in beautiful Kerala which is my favorite place with natural beauty.

If I go for holidays, I spend at least one week in this area. Since I am quite busy person with my work, this is the only time for me to interact with my family members. So I always want to spend these days only with my family members.

Last year, I went for a holiday for two weeks which was very interesting because we cooked food for ourselves on the road side and we also found some suitable places for having food. It was the first experience of such kind for me and I will never forget it. I am not good at cooking. But on those days I made different foods which were a whole new experience for me as well as for my family members. Actually we planned to buy foods from some restaurants. However, it did not work due to some reasons. Firstly, I felt very sad because of inconvenience. But later we managed very well and we enjoyed a lot. Still I cherish each and every moment with my relatives.

Sample Cue Card 26

> # Describe your favorite animal.
>
> **You Should Say:**
> - ➢ What kind of animal it is
> - ➢ Describe it briefly
> - ➢ Why do you like the animal
>
> **And describe why it is your favorite animal.**

Sample Answer 1:

Today I am going to tell you about my favorite animal, what it is, where it lives, when I first encountered it and why I like it so much.

I like lots of animals, so it is difficult to choose just one. However, I think my favorite animal is the Warthog. Warthogs live in Africa. They are a sort of wild pig. They get their name because they have four fleshy bumps on their faces, which look a bit like warts. These are part of the defense mechanism for males when they fight. Some people think warthogs are ugly, but I think they are lovely, they have great character.

I was lucky enough to spend some time volunteering at a property in South Africa. At the property, there were three young warthogs which had been orphaned after their mother was poached – killed for food. The baby warthogs were therefore hand-reared. When they were old enough, they were set free to run around in the wild. However, because they were so used to people they preferred to stay nearby.

These three warthogs were very friendly, intelligent and loved to play. They also like to follow their leader. In the wild, baby warthogs will run after their mothers, these three young hogs used to follow us. They would run after us even if we were in a vehicle or on a horse – once they even tried to follow the landowner when he took off in his helicopter. The pigs (*as we started to call them*) loved to be scratched and cuddled, they were very affectionate. They were also very nosy, whatever we did, and they wanted to be with us.

I love warthogs, they are energetic, loyal, and funny and I think they are beautiful too. Though I do understand the saying '*beauty is in the eye of the beholder*'.

Sample Answer 2:

My favorite animal is cow and it is much more beneficial than other animals. It gives us milk which is a nutritious protein supply for us. It provides us meat and the leather equipments are made from its skin. In some countries, the cow is used for plowing the land and for faming purposes. The teeth and bones of this animal are sometimes used to make comb, buttons and other useful things. In some areas, the dung is used as fertilizer and to burn fires.

The cow is a four footed animal and its skin is thick. Grass is its main food and they are mostly domestic animals. I like this animal mostly because of its closeness to human and its usefulness for us. In my childhood we had 5-6 cows at our home and they were very friendly. They had been very helpful for us. I like it as it is very gentle and sober animal. I also enjoy when I see a cow is ruminating and giving milk to her calf.

Sample Cue Card 27

Describe a child you know.

You should say:
   - ➢ Who the child is
   - ➢ How you know him/her
   - ➢ How you act with the child

And explain why you like/ dislike this child.

Sample Answer:

My grandfather had been the father of six children and later on when they became parents, the family grew up quite large. In our joint family there are several children and among them the youngest boy of my elder sister is the one I'd like to talk about. He is 3-4 years old and is my most favorite nephew. His name is Abraham and I call him Nir. I still remember the day he came in to this world and I chose to name him Abraham. He lives with his parents in a different city and they visit us almost 3-4 times each year.

From his childhood he was very cute and adorable. I loved him very much and because of my affection towards him, he became very fond of me. I usually see him with an interval of 3/4 months and each time I get the feeling that he has grown up more.

We often play hide-and-seek and cricket together with other people and kids. He loves to listen to the ghost stories, adventurous stories and fairy stories. While their stay at our home, he stays with me at night and I tell him bed time stories. We often go to walk in the field, go to open places like parks, near river and forest. He likes ice-cream and I buy him chips, ice-creams and chocolates. He loves sweet and hates to eat any pungent food. I often cuddle him, make fun with him and play with him. My affection and love for him is acute and I love to spend time with him.

Sample Cue Card 28

Describe a sporting event you attended.

You should say:
- ➢ What kind of sport event it was
- ➢ Give details of this event
- ➢ How often it takes place

And explain why you consider this event to be interesting.

Sample Answer 1:

I attended the Asia Cup final cricket tournament that was held at Dhaka Stadium in the year 2002 or 2003. We went to Dhaka to watch the game and stayed at a hotel during this time. I had 3-4 friends and a cousin with me from the very beginning. We had had our ticket almost 3 months before the game started. On the day we left the hotel early morning and took a taxi to reach near the stadium. We found a huge crowd there; in fact the crowd was much more than we anticipated and expected. I found one of my friends wearing the jersey of a team and others whistles. The crowd and their patience in the line gave the impression how much popular this game over here.

I had a flag with me of the team I supported. We had to stay in the line for about 45 minutes before we finally entered in to the stadium. I simply became overwhelmed with the sheer number of spectators and their festivity and support for the game.

The game started at 9.00 am and the people were enjoying it very much. The game was really enjoyable and I found supporters for both of the team. The crowd, the music, the competition, the excitement of the game, and the liveliness and spontaneous actions of the spectators were noteworthy. After the first team ended their innings, we went outside and were looking for a hotel to eat. But people were everywhere and there were no seat in the hotel. Finally we got an empty hotel after walking almost 20 minutes and sat there to have our lunch. We returned to the stadium in 35 minutes and the second innings started. Several TV channels were broadcasting the live game and the number of people watching this very game in the world would not be less that 70 million.

The first team scored 280 and that was a good fighting score at that time. The second team started hammering the bowls from the very beginning. It seemed to me that they would not need more than 30 overs to win the game. But they started losing wickets and in 20 overs they lost 3 wickets. The spirit and excitement of the spectators looked like a waving sea. The team I was supporting started doing really good. In the evening the game started turning in favor of the first team and became very close. Cricket is a game of uncertainty and this game became even more competitive and uncertain. Both team had the chance to win and the game was changing in every 10 minutes. The last 30 minutes were breathless and extremely exciting and finally the team I was supporting won the match.

This event takes place once in every two years and the schedule and venue is selected and maintained by the ICC. This was my first experience to visit Dhaka as well as watching such an exciting match. I have watched few other cricket matches in the stadium, but none of them was as exciting as this one was. The crowd, the enthusiasm of the people and the superb weather made it an interesting one.

Sample Answer 2:

Gosh, this topic is hard for me, I don't really go to many sporting events, and it isn't especially an interest of mine. However, I can think of one which enticed me to go and watch, I'll tell you as much as I can about the event, how often it takes places and why it was, to me at least, interesting.

The sporting event I went to was Le Tour de France – except it wasn't. For one year only the opening stages took place near to where I live in South Yorkshire, but more of that later.

The event is a world famous cycling race. It takes place every year, in a series of stages which are mainly in France, but it does occasionally pass through other countries. I think it started around 1903, and has taken place each year since then – apart from during the two world wars when obviously it was suspended. The cyclists are professional riders, and the tour is grueling. The route changes each year, but always includes both hilly and mountain stages, fast flat sections and covers a huge distance of some three and a half thousand kilometers over about 23 days. I am told there are about 20 teams or so each year, each with nine riders. To be honest I get very confused about how it is all timed and organized, but I do know that for each stage, the rider who has completed it in the fastest time gets to wear a yellow jersey for the next stage of the tour.

The race has fallen foul of cheating over the years, famously Lance Armstrong who won it some seven times I think was later banned for drug taking. However, more recently cycling has cleaned up its act and gained in popularity. In 2014, a decision was made to have the Grand Depart – the start of the Tour de France in South Yorkshire. This part of England where I live has fantastic scenery and very, very steep hills that were deemed suitably challenging of the super-fit and competitive cyclists. Although I've never previously been interested in cycling, some of my friends are, and with such a world famous event happening on my doorstep I wouldn't have wanted to miss out.

On the day of the race itself lots of roads were closed. I met up with some friends and we caught a tram as far out of the city as we could, and then walked the final stages to a good viewing point along the route. I had no idea what to expect but it was amazing. The weather was gorgeous, and Yorkshire and Sheffield folk had turned out in droves. I think about 2.5 million of us lined the route over the weekend it was passing through. I climbed up a bank and hung onto a tree to get a good vantage point as the cyclists raced through in the peloton (*a new word for me that I learned whilst spectating*). To be completely honest, the actual cyclists passed by in an instant, what made the event fun to watch were, the build-up and the atmosphere. The race was led by a convoy of floats and support vehicles. There was lots of good natured banter and sharing of food and snacks as the crowds waited for the bikes to come and plenty of people in hilarious fancy dress on French or cycling themes. Bunting was hanging everywhere, and brightly painted yellow bikes were scattered along the route. The weather showed off our Yorkshire hills and scenery at its very best, it was awesome.

I was really proud to be one of the supporters on what was a once in a lifetime opportunity to see The Tour de France passing through practically on my doorstep (*I live in Sheffield*). The race director for the event later described Yorkshire's Grand Depart as the "*grandest*" in the 111-year history of the race, it was wonderful to be part of that, it hasn't made me want to take up cycling though – those hills are ferocious.

Sample Cue Card 29

Describe a practical skill you have.

You should say:
- ➤ What the skill is
- ➤ How often you use it
- ➤ Who taught it to you

And explain how it helps you in your life.

Sample Answer:

The practical skill that I have is digital / computer designing. I had a passion on designing and art in my childhood and after my father bought me a computer when I was in class 8, I started my journey towards the designing.

I still remember that I started my painting on MS- Paint and later on I learned 2-3 major designing software namely Photoshop and Illustrator. I took 2 year's diploma course on designing and have worked for card, banner, poster, logo and web designing. Besides, I have learned how to create a webpage after designing it.

I have gained the skill by practicing a lot. I read different books on designing how to and concepts, spent numerous hours on designing and learned many things from the teachers who used to take our classes. I have learned many designing aspects, tips and tutorials from different design related websites as well.

Practice and the opportunity to work on several tasks helped me master the skill. I still need a long way to go and I am still a passionate designer. Besides my academic study, I still work on designing specifically on freelancing projects and that brings me a good amount of money.

I am sure this skill will help me do even better in the professional sector in the future.

Sample Cue Card 30

> # Describe something healthy you enjoy doing.
>
> **You should say:**
> - What you do
> - Where you do it
> - Who you do it with
>
> **And explain why you think doing this is healthy.**

Sample Answer:

I wake up early in the morning and then walk for an hour every day. After that I swim in the nearby river for about 30 minutes and then I start my day. Waking up very early and then doing the physical exercise is the healthy habit I have developed from the early stage of my life.

I remember my father insisting us to wake up very early and then took us to the nearby high school ground for exercise. Nowadays, I wake up from bed at around 6:00 am and wear my exercise trousers and the pair of shoes. Then I start walking along with the road that has passed beside the river. The fresh air in the morning is very healthy for health. Sometimes I take my bicycle and instead of walking, I ride my cycle. I started doing this early morning exercise and swimming few years back but nowadays 2 of my friends and cousins accompany me almost every day. They enjoy doing the exercise very much.

The morning is a time when the air and environment remain fresher than anytime of the day. So breathing the fresh air, doing the exercises and finally swimming in the fresh water is definitely a very healthy habit. A sound mind lies on a sound body and this habit that I adopted is pretty helpful for keeping a sound health and sound mind.

Sample Cue Card 31

Describe a game or sport you enjoy playing.

You should say:
> - What kind of game or sports it is
> - Who you play it with
> - Where you play it

And explain why you enjoy playing it.

Sample Answer:

I've played several games, both indoor and outdoor games, and still try to play whenever I get time. Among those games, I enjoyed playing chess more than others. Chess is an indoor game where two players participate. This game does not involve any major physical movements like other outdoor games but a chess player has to use his/her brain and make game plans to defeat the opponent.

I mostly play this game with my friends and cousins. Sometimes I play it with my father and senior relatives. Since playing chess requires only placing the board on a surface and sitting position of the two participating players, it is convenient to play chess almost anywhere. I mostly play it at our veranda, garden or bed room. I enjoy this game because I have a fascination about this game from my childhood and I really like the overall theme and barnstorming involved in this game. It's a thought provoking game that gives the participating players to use their brains. A player can apply his/her strategy, and then allure the opponent to fall in trap which is much like a real battle field.

It's not a game where someone would only use the physical movements rather the game requires perfect game plan, finding weakness of the opponent and a battle strategy. This game gives you a feel of being the King of a regime where you decide your country men's fate. For all those reasons this is a very interesting and enjoyable game to me.

Sample Cue Card 32

> ### Describe a memorable childhood experience.
>
> **You should say:**
> - ➤ Who was with you
> - ➤ Where it took place
> - ➤ What you did
>
> **And explain why it is memorable.**

Sample Answer:

Childhood is a time when everything is magical and pleasant. The possibility and dreams are vast and things become happier in childhood. Everybody has childhood memories and among them some are pleasant and some are sad. I have various childhood memories and I would like to talk about my childhood memory related to my first day at school.

I was about 6 years old when my parents got me admitted in a local school. I had a fascination of going to school from 3-4 years as I recall and when my father finally announced that I'll get admitted in the coming January, I felt like being in heaven.

I imagined school would be a great place and I would have lots of friends and I would study there. On the day, my parents took me to the school that I had saw many times from outside but never entered. After entering the school, I find myself anxious about everything.

I was unsure what to do, who to talk to, what to do when the teachers would ask questions and many such things. After my father submitted some necessary papers and fees to the admission department, they gave me new books, a temporary Identity Card and a syllabus. I started feeling comfortable after I found that some of our neighboring kids were already in this very school and they came to me and talked to me. This took place at my hometown where I grew up and I had been to this school for the next 4 years.

To my surprise one of the teachers asked my parents to leave me and told me to attend the classes. I was not at all prepared to join the class but I found I had little choice over that. My parents spent few times and advised me how to behave, how to listen to teachers and many more tips. After my parents abandoned me, I was frightened for few moments and sat at a corner of the class. The teacher asked to come forward and introduce myself. I found I was unable to walk and talk. But in few minutes my hesitation got away and I was talking about myself.

The teacher appreciated me and some of the new classmates came forward and greeted me. I started enjoying the class and teachers and found that I started loving my school. Later on I got admitted in college, university and many other places but the memory of first day at primary school was totally different and I still remember the day evidently.

> # Describe a life changing experience.
>
> **You should say:**
> - ➤ Where it took place & who was with you
> - ➤ What happened
> - ➤ How it made you feel
>
> **And explain how it changed your life.**

Sample Answer:

I was only 6 or 7 years old then and went to visit my grandpa in our village. I had lots of cousins and many of them were similar to my age. Visiting the village was very exciting to me. One day I along with my cousins went to play in the evening and all of a sudden we decided to catch some fished from the nearby pond. We had no hook or net to catch fishes so we decided to do it with our bare hands.

There were no people around so no one was there to warn us. As we did not know how to swim and had no idea about the depthless of the river, we lost control and all of a sudden I found that I and my cousin were trying to get out of the water. We already got ourselves trapped in the deep water and were struggling to breath. I barely remember what happened except that I was trying with my last effort to fight with water and get into the land. I can't recall how much time had spent but suddenly I found that I was lying on my mother's lap and was trying to find my cousin who faced the same fate as I did.

Later I heard that both of us were almost sinking in the water and an old woman came to rescue us. She was a village dweller who came to take water from the pond and had noticed us. She single handedly rescued me and then my cousin.

This event was a life changing event for me. After that event I learned how important it is to stay closer to parents and to heed to their advices. I also learned how fleeting our lives are and we out to help each other. From then I also started respecting all sort of people from all ages and always believed in human. When we are in danger, human (*known and unknown*) would come to rescue us. So we should never disrespect the human and always keep faith on them.

Tragic part is that, the grandson of the old woman who saved us died in the water of a river. Knowing it I started strongly believing in fates and then the tests we are bound to face in our lives.

Sample Cue Card 34

> **Describe something useful you learned from a member of your family.**
>
> **You Should Say:**
> - What you learned
> - How this became useful later in your life
> - Have you taught it to someone
>
> **And explain why it was important for you.**

Sample Answer:

I have been grown-up in a joint family with more than 10 family members. They were my parents, siblings, grandma, grandpa, uncle, aunt and cousins. I had the chance to learn so many things from them and it is in fact natural that a kid would learn things from his/her family members. I have learned swimming from my uncle, learned paining from my aunt, learned to play chess from my grandpa, learned to play cricket and badminton from my brother and so on and on. I have learned how to handle the stress and adverse time from my parents and learned how to behave with unknown people from my elder cousin. Thus the list would be a very long one. But I would like to emphasize the thing that I learned from my younger aunt and that is the reading habit and the pleasure of reading. Not that other things I learned from other family members are of less importance, but the reading for please and true interest of reading that I learned from my aunt is different and have a great power.

I found my aunt very charming, caring and possesses a great personality. She had been a voracious reader and because of that she was more learned and wise than people of her age. Initially I thought that how come she spend most of her time reading. Over the time I became close to her, and she started helping me with my studies. She started inspiring me to read books other than my academic books. She read me stories and that help me grow an interest towards books. Then she started telling me amazing stories of our history and showed me which books actually have those histories written.

She shared the stories she were reading and thus we started becoming good critic of stories and writers. She told me more stories that I have heard from anyone else. I am grateful to her that she so painstakingly explained different topics and help me grow a good interest on reading. Because of her contribution I have started reading books of different types whenever I got time which I think is a better investment and activity than spending time idly.

Later I have inspired my nephew to read book. I did the same; I read him stories which would be interesting to him and gave him sweets, candies, ice-cream if he could have finished a book and explain the stories. I guess he has become interested in reading as well.

Sample Cue Card 35

> # Describe a river or a sea you have visited.
>
> **You should say:**
> - Where the river/ sea was
> - What activities you did there
> - Who was with you
>
> **Explain why you liked this particular place and why do you recommend the place for others to visit.**

Sample Answer:

I have once been at Cox's Bazar for about a week and really enjoyed my visit there. Cox's Bazar is considered to be the largest sea beach in the world and it is beside the Bay-of-Bengal. We had the trip to visit the sea, beach and natural beauty of this place.

Three of our friends including me went there in 2012 probably around June. This was a good time to visit the sea beach. We stayed at hotel which was very close to the sea. We could hear the roaring sounds of the sea from our hotel especially at night. The sea seems endless and this was my first time to see the vastness of the sea. I tried to imagine the position of the other shore of the sea and the depth of it and after sometimes abandoned this silly idea. I was really surprised when we took a motor-boat to visit a nearby island. All I could see was water around us. The waves were so enormous and high that I thought this would hit us hard and our boat would sink. I am not ashamed to disclose that I was bit frightened about the big waves and our small boats.

At night I walked beside the sea, I watched the lives surrounding the sea, people and their culture. The moon looked like a hanging light in the wall on the other side of the sea. The sea looked less formidable at night except the sound which was louder at night. The people, tourists from different locations, local people, fishermen, the long sea beach and the sea exposed a life and place that we never knew about. I enjoyed fresh foods and fishes, different culture of people, the vastness of the sea, the hotel, the working class people and their mildness and have planned to visit the place again whenever possible.

Sample Cue Card 36

Describe one of your neighbors.

You Should Say:
- ➤ When you two become neighbors
- ➤ Do you often meet
- ➤ State whether your neighbor is a good person

And explain why you like/ dislike this neighbor.

Sample Answer 1:

I'm lucky, I've got good neighbors. I'm going to tell you about just one of them, when we met, how often we meet and why I think he is a good neighbor who I like very much.

I live in an old house which has been converted into about eleven different flats and bedsits. I live on the top floor, which is actually the modernized attic space of the original building. There is just one other flat in this roof area. To get to my flat, and that of my immediate next door neighbor, you have to go up a back stairway that was probably originally the servants' staircase, I think what is now my flat and that of my neighbor's too, must have been at one time servants' quarters. This means that our doorways are directly opposite one another, and we are the only people who use this entrance to the building.

I moved into the flat I live in about four or five years ago now. It is a rented flat. At that time the flat opposite me was empty, but a few weeks later I met a woman a little bit older than me who was busy cleaning just inside the flat, but with the door wide open. I paused to introduce myself and talk to her. She was really friendly, and I found out it was her son who was to be my new neighbor. She was just helping him to move in. A bit later he, Steve, turned up too. He was new to the area, so I explained where all the local shops were, when the rubbish was taken out and various other little details about the practicalities of living in the property. A couple of days later he knocked on my door and called round for a chat. We found we got on really well. We have a very similar sense of humor, a shared (*but slightly half-hearted*) interest in running, and a mutual appreciation of good food – I could recommend the deli over the road to him as a source of lovely upmarket cheeses, olives and home-made lasagna and delicious pasta and pesto sauce too. We also both have an unfulfilled wanderlust, always plotting our next journey. He is off to Australia soon, lucky him.

Given how close we live together, our front doors face directly onto one another, we see each other incredibly rarely. We both have busy lives, working full time but different hours. At weekends I tend to be out and about, and he'll often disappear for the weekend to stay with his girlfriend. Even so, whenever we do meet, it is always friendly, we make each other laugh. We often end up having long conversations just chatting in the hallway outside our front doors. I probably see him only once a fortnight or so, but we leave each other notes too from time to time if we need help with anything.

Steve is a great neighbor, because I know I could call on him if I needed to. We will always help each other if we can. I dug his car out of the snow for him once as he didn't have a shovel, but he's returned the favor in other ways, taking in parcels for me when I'm away for example. Because I live on my own it is really important to me to have a neighbor close by that I trust and like. I was really sad when he told me he was planning to emigrate. I was also really pleased for him. You have to wish someone well when they are following their dreams. I hope my new next-door neighbor is half as nice.

Sample Answer 2:

Mr. Andrew John (*use a common name of your country*) is one of the neighbors whom I like very much. Since I live in an urban area, people are close to each other and maintain a strong neighborhood relationship unlike the metropolitan area.

In our neighbor, we know almost each and every people living there, what they do, what are their updates, what are their profession and their overall personality and characteristics as well. Mr. John's house is adjacent to ours and I meet him almost every day. Mr. John is a retired army person who is now around 55 years old. He lives in his house alone and I have never found his relatives visiting him except some old colleagues. He stays inside his house most of the time and in the evening he sits in the veranda. He is a quiet man and likes to read a lot. I have seen him coming to live in his house almost 5-6 years ago. He bought the house from our previous neighbor.

I had had several conversations with him and I often play chess with him. I like to read as well and our reading habit was the primary reason we started liking our accompany each other. I like and admire this man very much. Though at first impression he seems to be an arrogant person, but in reality he is an intelligent, calm, good-hearted and charming man. I have heard lots of stories from him. He has travelled to many different places and has lots of experience. Since I have become close to him, he refer me books that I mostly enjoy reading. He advises me whenever I seek for his guidance. He is sometimes a close friend, sometimes a mentor and sometimes a guardian. I like him because of our unclaimed friendship, his personality, honestly, morality and his great mind.

Tell me about your most favorite music band.

You should say:
- What is it and why do you like it
- How do people react to the music of this band
- When you first heard their song

And explain the necessity of listening music.

Sample Answer:

There are many music bands that I like very much but Pink Floyd is my most favorite music band. This band is a famous music band for their music which falls under the genre progressive rock, psychedelic rock and art rock. Though the band is not active anymore yet they are heard by millions of music lovers. They are basically English rock band that was founded in 1965 and remained active till 1995 and reunited in 2005. I have become a big fan of this band mostly because of their distinguished philosophical lyrics, sonic experiment and mind-blowing music quality.

The Pink Floyd is considered to be one of the most musically influential and commercially successful bands of all time. Their albums have been sold well over 250 million records worldwide. Regarding the question how people react to their music, it depends on the listener and their choice of music but people good music choice and quality lyrics choice are bound to love the songs of this band. Each of their album got high appraisal from the music critic and their album "*The Wall*" is widely known all over the world.

I have first listened to their music (*most probably songs from the album 'Atom hearted mother'*) when I was in my 11th grade of school and after than I have listened to almost all of their songs countless times.

There are many reasons we should listen to music. It is considered to be the food of soul. Music is refreshing and washes away the tiredness, boredom and monotonousness.

Good lyrics help us brainstorm, understand things more deeply and from different perspectives, and help grow positive inspiration and motivation. Music inspires us deeply and eliminates our boredom and narrowness in life. It is one of the best entertainments and inspirational sources for human being.

Sample Cue Card 38

> ## Describe your Favorite Shopping Mall /A Shopping Mall you often visit.
>
> **You should say:**
> - What's the name and location it
> - How often do you go there and what do you buy from there
> - What types of people usually go there
> - Describe the Shopping Centre

Sample Answer:

I am from Ho Chi Minh City and I like the Diamond Plaza shopping mall that I often visit. It is best known as the Diamond Plaza and is situated at 34, Le Duan Street, near the Notre Dame Cathedral. I visit this shopping mall almost twice in a month and sometimes more frequent than that.

People from nearby places and from the city are the most frequent visitors but it's not uncommon that tourists and shoppers from other cities come and shop from this shopping mall. This shopping center includes a 22 story building plus an adjacent 15 story building and offers a great shopping experience including restaurants, cafe, hospital, lounges, Cinema Theater. There is a helicopter pad on the roof of this mall and offers many other facilities.

The Diamond Plaza shopping mall hosts many renowned brands and offers distinctive shopping experience. You can find almost everything you need to shop from here. Many fashion fans find it as their prime place for shopping and the shopping environment is unmatched. One does not need to be rich to come and shop here as the goods offered suits the people from economic status.

The food court is something you would love about this shopping mall. There are more than hundreds of food shops that you can pick from and the game center attracts mostly the game lovers and teenagers. The movie theater of the Diamond Plaza is called Lotte Cinema and is in the 13th floor. With the most modern facility and safe environment this is an ideal shopping center for all types of shoppers.

I like this shopping mall mostly because of the quality products and good price offering. Apart from that the security, customer service and nice environment also attract me. Another reason that affects my shopping decision from this shopping mall is its distance from my living place. It takes only 15 minutes to reach there and this is one of the reasons I mostly decide to shop there.

Sample Cue Card 39

Describe a city you have visited /describe your favorite city.

You should say:
- ➢ What is the name and where is it
- ➢ When you visited it
- ➢ Why did you like it
- ➢ What are the attractive places of this city

And explain what influence the city had on you.

Sample Answer:

Sydney is my most favorite city among the cities I have visited. Sydney is the state capital of New South Wales of Australia. This city is situated in the bank of Tasman Sea and has around 4.6 million people. I have visited this city in 2009, after I finished my graduation and loved my stay there. Sydney had many attractive natural area, botanic garden, parks, and high rising buildings. This city has many heritage listed building that attracts the tourists and visitors. The Sydney Opera House is one of the most recognized landmarks in Australia and is a great place to visit.

This city is known for the dynamic cultural hub and it has many famous museum, galleries and art galleries as well. Because of the great architecture, warm weather and hundreds of tourists attraction more than 11 million international and domestic tourists visit this city each year. I had been there for about 14 days and I really enjoyed everything about this city. I stayed at a 20 storied hotel that offered a really amusing sight views. The transportation system of the city is better than many other cities and I could have been maintaining the track and time of my schedules because of that. I loved being at open & wide spaces in the gardens and parks. People are welcoming and friendly there. A tourist can get plenty of helps both from people and the authority and can roam easily without any interruption. I saw 2/3 art museum and some cultural festivals and those were awesome.

There are so many places to be, so many things to do in Sydney. Some of the attractive places are, Royal Botanic Garden, Hyde Park, Queen Victoria Building, Sydney Town hall, Macquarie Lighthouse, Australia Square, Sydney Opera House and many more.

I had a tremendous vacation in Sydney and I liked most of the places there and I enjoyed so much that I did not even notice how quickly the 2 weeks scheduled time has passed.

Sample Cue Card 40

> # Describe a place that you like to go.
>
> **You should say:**
> - Where the Place is
> - How you get there
> - What it looks like
>
> **And explain why you like this place.**

Sample Answer 1:

There are lots of places I like to go, depending on my mood. Today I'm going to tell you about a special place near to where I live. I will explain where it is and how I get there. I will try and describe what it looks like and explain why I like the location so much.

I am lucky, although I live in a city, from my house I can walk to the edges of the Peak District, which is a beautiful national park just a few miles from the city center. To get to the national park I have to walk from my house down some local roads, and up a steep hill past some allotments. After about a mile or so striding out away from the urban areas, I get to a lovely bit of woodland which has a public footpath you can follow onwards and upwards. It can be a bit of a scramble towards the end of the path as it is very steep indeed, but eventually you leave the woodland and are on the edge of open farm land. Another footpath crosses some sheep-filled fields, and finally you are on the moors of the Peak District. It is really spectacular.

The Peak District can be a really wild place, with its vast expanses of open moorland. You are high up, and it is quite exposed so it can be very windy and cold even in the summer. There are rocky outcrops and strange configurations of stones that have been weathered by centuries of wind and rain to create dramatic shapes. Some boulders are in piles, and there are steep vertical cliffs too. The area attracts lots of people who like walking, climbing and bouldering because of its unique and beautiful landscape. Everywhere is dark wet peat under foot, and lots of heather. This is a low growing plant that flowers at the end of the summer turning the whole landscape purple. The park covers a huge area, I think around 555 square miles, so the terrain differs from area to area, of course I am biased, but I believe I live near the most remarkably beautiful part.

I love this place, because if ever I am feeling down, or a bit enclosed, in just an hours walk I can find myself in a deserted but picturesque place, where the elements are more extreme. In winter rain and wind can batter you, but in summer the sky seems to go on forever. Every day is different up there, and every hour of every day too. The area is so huge, that often you can have it all to yourself, of course there are other walkers about, but you can quickly disappear in the vastness of the space. The people, who live in Sheffield, like me, are very proud that we are so near to the Peak District National Park, and it is no surprise it became the United Kingdom's first national park on 17 April 1951. A birthday that should be celebrated I think.

Sample Answer 2:

I like to visit my hometown more than visiting any other place. After I finished my school, I came to the capital of your country and did my graduation here. Later on, I have started my job and since then have been staying here. Whenever I get vacations, I plan to visit my hometown.

To go there, I need to purchase advance bus ticket 2-3 days prior to the departure. I mostly go there by bus. Alternatively, I can go to my hometown on train. The bus journey takes around 4-5 hours and the train journey takes 1-2 hours more than the bus journey. After reaching at our hometown station, I usually pick a shared taxi that drops me near my home.

My home town is a small urban area with full of beauty and wonder. Green trees, fresh air and serene environment make it an ideal place to live in. My hometown is just beside a river and has less density of population than the capital city. The houses and shopping centers are not crammed and have their own urban charms. My hometown is a special place for me as I have spent my childhood there. There are three tourist attractions are there and the place is renowned for traditional foods and customs. Roads are clean and people are educated there. Anyone who would this place would find it attractive.

Sample Cue Card 41

Tell a childhood story you heard when you were a kid.

You should say:
- ➤ Who told you the story
- ➤ What was the story
- ➤ Why you liked it

And explain why you have remembered the story.

Sample Answer 1:

Childhood stories were fascinating and in my childhood I had been very fond of those short of stories. My grandmother used to tell me stories before going to sleep. One such childhood story that I can remember is about a prince who fought and defeated a mighty giant to rescue his princess.

He was a good prince who helped his countrymen and was a very good fighter. He was happily married with the prince he fall in love with. They were benevolent kings and queens for the country and people of the country loved them very much. One day a giant ghost came from other territory and tried to abduct a small kid. The prince was out of the country at that moment for business purpose and the queen tried to force the giant to leave. That irritated the giant and it finally abducted the queen. The prince returned to the country few days back and learned the stories. He became very gloomy and decided to search for his queen. Everybody tried to protest him but he finally remain steady on his decision. He started a long and struggle-some journey to find the giant and rescue the queen. The journey was much surprising and full of different puzzles and obstacles. He finally reached to the abyss and found the queen. He had to fight with the giant and finally kill it to get his princess back.

As a kid this was one of my very favorite stories. My grandma told me the story multiple times and I used to insist her to tell me this very story. As a kid the story opened new horizon to me. I believed that every word of this story was true and that's why it made a special place in my mind. Most probably I have thought a lot about the things happened in this story and as a result I have still remembered the story.

Sample Answer 2:

My mother used to tell me bed-time stories in my childhood and I have heard some of those stories so many times they have been permanently depicted in my memory.

One such story was the story of a boy who was 10 years old and got lost one day. The boy tried to get back home but since a bad magician used his black magic on the boy, he could not get back to home. The boy would be totally lost once the magic engulf him totally and the magician would then use the boy to do bad things. But in the boy's memory was his mother and father and that's why he was not totally lost. The boy continue his search for the way back to his home and on this journey he met an old man, a wounded tiger, a candy man, a king and a nomad with gold coins. Each time the boy met someone many exciting things happened. In fact those were the tests for him. If he passes those tests would be able to get back home and if he fails the tests, he would never be able to get back home. His confront with the king was most exciting as he had to go to different places and collect different things from challenging places to prove that he was innocent. Each time the boy faced a new challenge and amazing circumstances, the story gets more exciting.

After the boy won the last challenge he was given, the impact of the magic was no longer applicable and he found that he was standing nearby his home. As a kid I really enjoyed the story. I was almost the same age the boy in the story was and every time he faced a new challenge, the story took a turn and revealed another challenges. The story was intelligently made and I loved to hear it.

Sample Cue Card 42

Describe a relative whom you like.

You should say:
  - ➤ Who the relative is and how close you are to him/ her
  - ➤ What makes you like your relative
  - ➤ What do you do together

And describe why this person is close to you.

Sample Answer 1:

I like many of my relatives and among them I'd like to pick my Grandma whom I really love and admire. She is a loving woman who always loves me. She lives with us and very close to me. I share lots of my own stuffs with her. She cares me like a mother does for her own kids. She tells me stories, some of her own and some of them are from her young time. She has a good heart and she is nice to others.

In the morning she wakes me up and we go out for morning walk. All of our family members take our breakfast together. Sometimes I read her books and watch religious TV programs together. Sometimes I urge my wish to her and then she bargains it with my parents. In a way she is a very close friend of mine.

My grandma is very fond of me and I like her very much as well. We have a good bonding between us that makes our relationship easy and soothing.

Sample Answer 2:

I like many of my relatives who are very compassionate, lovely and friendly to me and among them I would pick my younger uncle as the best relative in terms of our mutual understanding, closeness and communications. In fact, we share so many common interest and activities that he is more like a friend to me than a guardian. I am very close to him and we share our books, thought and views on different issues like two close friends would do.

I like him because of his authentic compassion, support for me and because of the common interest he shares with me. I personally find him very benevolent and talented and he is a good counselor for me. I respect him and it surprises me the way he treats me. I have never found him to ignore me and treat me as a younger nephew ever and that's something I really like about him.

We often discuss our family issues, our thoughts of the politics, religion, books writers, movies, music and on many other issues. We share our books and recommend books to each other. I find his taste very much similar to me and that makes us do lots of things together including travelling, watching movies, spending holidays together and many more activities someone would like to do with friends. He even spends time with my friends without any hesitation.

I am the only child of my parent and from my childhood I found that my younger uncle was living in our house. This was the main reason we became close and apart from that the shared interests, his personality and behavior actually made us close. He took care of me in my childhood and supported me in many ways in my teenage and with time I became very close to him.

Sample Cue Card 43

> # Describe a trip you have taken recently.
>
> **You should say:**
> - ➤ Where you went
> - ➤ Who went with you
> - ➤ Why you went there
>
> **And describe some things you saw and did on your trip.**

Sample Answer:

Few days back we went to (*tell a name of a place that you would like to talk about*) in an official trip. This trip was arranged by our office and all of our colleagues and some of their relatives went there. As it was an official tour and I had been thinking about going to such a trip, I agreed to go. The place was a good picnic spot and historically important. I have had plans to visit the place and when I heard that an official tour has been arranged there, I simply agreed to go to the trip without giving any second thought.

On the trip day all of the participants met at our office ground and took our seats on the bus. It was about 3-4 hours journey and at 10:30 am we reached at the spot. We visited the small museum there, took bath in a pond, ran through the narrow roads and bridged, climbed at small hills, played cricket, took photos, took our meals, arranged a singing competition, raffle draw program and many more interesting things there. We saw historical significance and documentary on a wide screen projector arranged by the governing authority of the place, we visited a small museum, and we saw fishes in the rivers, birds on the trees and many eye catching sceneries there. We stayed there whole day and returned home after the evening. That was a good trip that I really enjoyed.

Sample Cue Card 44

Describe an irritating neighbor of your locality.

You should say:
- For how long the person has been your neighbor
- How this person behave with others
- Explain how annoying the person is

And explain what can be done to reduce his annoying activities.

Sample Answer:

Most of our neighbors are amiable and well-behaved and they are good neighbors except Mr. Steve who seems very irritating to me. He is living in our community for about 4 years after he bought the house from the previous owner. So he is our neighbor for the last three years and shortly after he started living here people started noticing his annoying behaviors.

He is a retired person who has only 4 family members and though other family members are well-behaved, this person has some issues that make him a bad neighbor. He does not behave politely and often we find him rude with others. He often shouts on very silly issues. Even with kids he behaves rudely.

He often complaints about people standing in front of his house while it is a street and people stand there for a while to look for an auto. In my opinion he has no right to yell with the neighbors who play in the nearby playground. He does not go out very often and stays at his home most of the time. But he complains about everything, about everyone. Since he has complaints on other people, he should have followed the strict rules not to disturb others but in reality he does the opposite. He sometimes shouts with his family members that other people can hear and that's very disturbing especially in the middle of the night.

I remember him scolding an 8 years girl who mistakenly entered in his garden and just enjoyed the flowers. She did nothing and Mr. Steve acted very impolitely with her. People in our locality sometimes make fun of him for his behaviors and usually avoids him from social gathering. He has a habit of advising people while he does not listen to anybody's request. Thus I find him very annoying.

I am not sure what to do to reduce his annoyance but I guess we should talk to him very politely and try to make peace with him. He is not a type of person who would yield to logic or good intension. So if he does not heed to polite conversation, the local senior persons can sit with him to short out the problem. His family members can contribute to make him understand that the way he behaves with others are not acceptable and is not a good sign. Finally if nothing can be done to change him, we should avoid him and ignore his disturbance. He is not a kid whom we can teach the basic of mannerism and social responsibilities. So in my opinion a polite discussion can be effective and if not there is nothing we can do to change his behaviors.

Sample Cue Card 45

> ### Describe something you plan to learn in the future.
>
> **You should say:**
> - What you plan to learn in the future
> - Why you want to learn it
> - Where and how you will learn it
>
> **And explain why you have planned to learn it.**

Sample Answer 1:

I have a long desire to learn how to play a piano. Even after my desire and passion, I have not been able to learn it. If I ever get the time and opportunity to learn it, I would grab the chance.

I am not sure exactly when this passion grew in me, but I can guess it was something that came in my mind after I saw a foreign movie where an actor played this instrument. The movie was related to a musician's life and he mostly played piano and sang songs.

In the movie the actor played the piano 3-4 times and the quality of the music was really good. Possibly from that time the passion started to grow in my mind. I work as a computer programmer and have no intension to do any serious type music, but I want to learn to play the piano. If I get spare time and my schedule allows me, I will get admitted in a piano lesson in my city. Not many opportunities are there but I heard that there are 2/3 musicians who teach enthusiast people the piano for a high payment. I will probably get admitted in such a program and would keep learning.

I will need to save around $1000 to get admitted in to the piano lesson and hopefully will have this amount at the end of next year. Then I will talk to the musicians who offer the lesson and would pick one to learn from. I'll allow me to be free at least 2 days in a week to participate in the lesson and I would practice at least for an hour daily.

I know it takes a great determination, passion and talent to learn a creative thing like piano, but I believe, I will be able to achieve it.

Sample Answer 2:

I would say I want to learn computer programming in the future. More specifically, I want to learn C# (*C Sharp*) and PHP which are two very common yet powerful programming languages. Besides I want to enhance my skill in database programming so that I can combine those skills to develop great desktop and web based software and applications.

I come from commerce background and I have finished my undergraduate degree in business studies. During my 4th and 5th terms in the university, I got admitted in a computer training center and learned the basic of computing and programming. At that time I was introduced to the C programming language and I found that being able to write codes to develop a software is a great and unique skill. I found that I was coding very passionately at that time and I came to the decision that I would spend at least a year to learn programming. I want to learn it to enhance my skill, to get a job in Information Technology field and to develop some great software. Without knowing these programming languages, I will not be able to develop those applications and software.

Though I have learned some basic of C programming language, there are still so many things that I do not know about programming. As computerization is a must in every field of work, I want to prepare myself for this in advance. I need to learn more about programming to meet the great demands of the application of the computer.

I have decided to get admitted in a large IT training institute in our city and I would get enrolled in programming language courses. Besides, I would invest a great deal of my personal time to practice and would take help from Internet to become an advanced programmer. Online video tutorials and podcasts on learning to code would make things easier for me, I believe.

As I have already told, I want to build up my career in Information Technology related field and without learning those programming languages, it would be quite impossible for me. I want to develop some great software and make a great contribution in this field. Honestly I am quite ready to dedicate my time and effort to achieve this.

Sample Cue Card 46

Describe an interest or hobby that you particularly enjoy.

You should say:
- What is it
- How long have you been doing it
- Who you do it with

And explain why this is important to you.

Sample Answer 1:

Today I am going to talk about a hobby I particularly enjoy when I am at home in the UK. I will tell you what the hobby is, how long I have been doing it, who I do it with and why it is important to me.

My hobby is running! I know I do not really look like a runner, and it is true I am not very fast, but this is still the activity that I like to do in my spare time. I have not been running for very long. I started running just 18 months ago, as I decided I needed to get fit, and I thought it would be a cheap way to exercise. I did not expect to enjoy myself. Near to where I live there is a park. It is very beautiful with trees and streams. Each Saturday a large group of about 500 people meet at 9.00 a.m. in the morning, and go for a 5 km run together. This event is called Parkrun, and it happens in over 300 different places in the UK each week. I was nervous when I first went, but found the group was friendly and encouraging. Now I go every week, and I even have trained for some longer races 10 km and my longest was 20 km.

I have made lots of friends through running. However, the best surprise was that when I went to my local Parkrun, I met someone I had not seen for over 30 years. We had been at school together, but did not keep in touch. We had both moved to the new city of Sheffield and did not realize we lived so close to each other. Now I run with this friend every week, and we go for breakfast each Saturday after our run.

Running is important to me because it keeps me fit, has helped me make new friends, and it has shown me that I am not too old to try new things. I hope you all find activities that you enjoy doing in your spare time.

Sample Answer 2:

Blogging is the interest or hobby that I really enjoy and have been doing it very passionately for the last 2-3 years. Blog is basically the short form of 'weblog' and it lets the blogger write on topic she/he likes. It is very similar to a website and the blog posts I write is open for anyone to read using internet. The blogging I am doing is not collaborated with anyone else and I am alone maintaining and updating it.

The blog I am maintaining has lots of importance both for me and for the intended readers. For me, the blog helps me improving my writing skill as it requires lots of content writing, helps me exploring of relevant topics that improves my knowledge and to upload the images I take with my camera. Sometimes I write on how-to and tutorials which are helpful for people looking for it. Sometimes I write on books I read, movies I watch or about new things I learn and that helps me observing those in a different perspective. People can comment on the articles I add and thus I have got many others in my blog who shares similar interest that I have. Thus the importance of my blog immense to me and I maintain my blog with utmost passion and fervor.

For writing blog posts I need to explore different topics and thus this habit helps me increase my knowledge on different topics.

Sample Answer 3:

Today I am going to talk about an activity that I do in my spare time. I will explain what the hobby is; how long I have been doing it; who I do it with and why it is important to me.

I don't think you will be able to guess what my hobby is because it is quite unusual. In my free time I work at an Alpaca Farm. An alpaca is an animal that is kept for its fleece. They look a little bit like sheep but with a very long neck. They are related to camels and llamas which you may recognize more easily. They usually live in South America, but there is an Alpaca Farm near to me in Sheffield and I work there at weekends. Although it is called an Alpaca Farm, in fact there are lots of different animals there. Horses, goats, sheep, some ducks and hens and even some llamas.

Working with the alpacas and the other animals on the farm means I have to get there early in the morning. I help to feed the animals and clean up after them. Sometimes I have to drive a tractor to take hay and water out to the horses. Often there are visitors to the farm and I will give them a guided tour and introduce them to all the different animals. At some times of year I help with special jobs to care for them, such as giving injections to protect them from illnesses or trimming their toenails if they get too long. My favorite time of year to help is in the spring when baby Alpacas are born. New-born alpacas have to stand up very quickly and within hours are drinking milk from their mothers and running around – it is amazing to watch.

I work on the farm with the farm manager. He is a very kind and funny man. Although we might not seem to have much in common on the surface, we get on really well together. We laugh and talk all the time whilst we are getting the jobs done.

Although my hobby is unusual it is very important to me. My full time job is in indoors in an office and a lot of the time I am sitting down, so at weekends I like to get outside into the country side and do some physical work that is completely different. I love the animals, the fresh air and the exercise. I also really enjoy talking with the farm manager as he can tell great stories. In the winter though it can be very cold, and trudging through 3 foot of snow to feed the animals is really exhausting. On those days I am glad that working with the Alpacas is just a hobby, I can spend the rest of the week in the warm.

> ## Describe a difficult thing you did well.
>
> **You should say:**
> - What it was
> - How you did it
> - Why it was difficult
>
> **And explain how you felt after you did it.**

Sample Answer:

In our life, we do so many difficult things knowingly and unknowingly. For some difficult tasks, we get appreciation and some remain unnoticed by others. I would like to describe one of the difficult jobs I did and was appreciated as well. It was an event when I was around 16 years old and saved a little boy who was drowning in a pond. That day I was near a big pond of our town and all of a sudden I noticed a human hand in the water. No other part of the little boy's body could be seen except his hand that he was desperately trying to get up at the last moment of his life. Initially, I thought that I was just hallucinating and nothing was in the water but instantly I changed my mind and had been sure that it was a boy who was drowning. I took off my shoes and jumped into the water. Then I realized my mistake that I have not pointed out the exact place where I thought someone was sinking.

I desperately swam and went to the approximate place after I struggled for few minutes. But there was none to be found. I started feeling very helpless and found some people were looking at me with curious eyes. I shouted that I saw a boy was drowning and trying to save him. I found 2-3 others also get into the water to find the boy. I felt overwhelmed with the urge to find the boy. All of a sudden I saw the flash on water and quickly reached there. I felt someone who I had felt with my body and I tried to pull out him from the water. But to my surprise, it seems impossible to me to bring the boy out of the water.

I used all of my force, energy and determination and will to get the boy from the water. I had to struggle a lot and I was sure how long it took me to bring him up. To me, it seemed like an eternity and finally I had been able to grab the boy firmly and swam towards the land. I was worried because the boy had already lost his conscience and I tried my best to help him to breath. I pulled down and up my hands very strongly over his chest and finally he coughed. I felt very tired and yet happy that the boy was out of danger. Some people came to extend their helping hands and they took the boy to the nearby hospital. I went to the hospital and returned home when the boy was completely safe.

I felt real proud to be able to save the boy and the gratefulness I saw in the boy's parents is something I will never forget. People appreciated my bravery and efforts and I also felt very relieved and proud.

Sample Cue Card 48

A product you bought and dissatisfied about.

You should say:
- ➢ What was the product
- ➢ From where did you buy it
- ➢ What was not satisfying

And explain what you did about the product.

Sample Answer:

It would be probably 1 year or so when I bought a cell phone and went through a horrible experience. I bought Nokia C5 cell phone from a Nokia shop of the city shopping mall. I saved the amount to purchase a cell phone over 6 months that would allow me to use internet and install applications. Due to my budget deficiency I though Nokia C5 would be a good choice and the salesman also convinced me to purchase this particular one. I spent almost half an hour to test the phone before purchasing it.

I used the cell phone for about a month and I was very happy of its performance. It was touch phone and mostly operated with fingertip. All of a sudden one day I noticed that the touch functionality is not working and hence I am unable to use it and do anything. I restarted the phone and I found it okay again. But that problem kept reappearing over and over again and I took the phone to the service center. After a week I took back it home and used smoothly for 2 weeks or so and sadly the problem reappeared. That was a very frustrating experience and I explained my daunting experience to the customer care officer and he assured that they would fix it. But to my surprise I found the problem again. That day I decided to through it in the dustbin and bought a new cell phone by a different brand and manufacturer. Though I have not thrown it away to the dustbin, I placed it in a box with old and unused materials. I later bought a new cell phone by Sony and found it really cool.

Sample Cue Card 49

Describe your first day at work or the place where you study.

You should say:
- ➢ What kind of building was it located in
- ➢ Why was it important for you to work/study there
- ➢ How did you feel at the end of the first day

And explain if you were pleased or disappointed with the experience.

Sample Answer:

I am currently working in a company and I still remember the first day of my job. This is my second job and I have worked for the first company for about 2 years. After I finished my graduation I applied in some companies and was interviewed by them. One day I got a call from the HR head of the company that, I have been hired and expected to join them from the next Sunday. I was very excited and happy to get the job.

I did my preparation part to start the office and reached the office 30 minutes earlier. The office was in a 10 story building and the office was on the 6th floor. They had more than 100 employees. This was a modern building with a big yard in front it.

Then I contacted the HR head and submitted my academic and other relevant documents. The HR asked me to sit on a couch and after 30 minutes or so, he returned. In the meantime, I noticed other employees arrived and went to their work desks. Most of them looked at me and one person asked me if I am waiting for someone. I explained that I was joining from that day and he congratulated me. I was feeling a little bit nervous and noticed that heart was beating faster. The messenger came to me and offered me a cup of coffee. After the HR head came back, he gave 2-3 forms including the contact papers and asked me to read them all and fill up the forms. I read the papers and filled up the forms and gave it to the HR. The HR then took me to some of the key employees and introduced me to them. Then he showed me my desk and I sat over there. Since this was the first day of my office, I did not have any particular task. I started feeling easy after I sat on the desk and started using the computer. The computer was pre-configured and I went through the company website and learned lots of new information about their service and product offerings.

I took my lunch in a nearby cafeteria and came back to my desk again. Thus the clock ticked to 5:30 pm and I noticed others were leaving. I asked the HR and left with some of the employees.

I felt very comfortable at the end of the day and the hesitation I had has been removed and I was happy for the reason that the office environment and colleagues were very friendly.

Sample Cue Card 50

> # Talk about a peaceful place that you like.
>
> **You should say:**
> - Where is the place located
> - What is this place
> - How did you come to know about the place
>
> **And explain why you like that place.**

Sample Answer:

My grandfather's house is a peaceful place that I visit around 2-3 times a year and like very much. This is in the village (*say a village name*). My grandfather's house is a big house with lots of open spaces and a river is flowing nearby.

In this big house only 3-4 people and 2-3 servants live as my grandparents are no longer in this world and my uncles, aunts are mostly living in different big cities.

There are 7-8 rooms in the house and a big garden in front of the house. The servants take care of the garden and keep the place neat and clean. Since I live in a city and work for a big company where I have lots of responsibilities to perform, the city life seems very busy and even sometimes chaotic to me.

Whenever I visit my grandfather's house, I get an impression that I have come to the most peaceful place in the world. I have not seen many places and have not travelled extensively but in my experience the peace and the mental tranquility I enjoy being here are unmatched. One of the reasons can be my childhood memories as I have spent my childhood at this very house and whenever I go there, lots of memories flash back and give me a pleasure that I do not get from elsewhere.

I know this place from my childhood as I was born and grown up here. This place is different to me. I leave behind my busy life and come here to relax both mentally and physically. The memory of my departed grandparents, my childhood and other happy events are related to this place. I can get fresh air, meet some of my relatives, enjoy the country life and stay close to nature here and for all those reasons, I like this place very much.

Sample Cue Card 51

> ## Talk about a funny incident that happened to you.
>
> **You should say:**
> - What it was
> - Why it was funny
> - Who was there with you
>
> **And what you remember most about it.**

Sample Answer:

The funny incident that I remember happened was almost 3 years ago that I would like to describe.

That time I was a student in a university and I was in my 7th semester. We had a group assignment and to collect data we went to some libraries after our class. In the evening, I found that my group members are complaining that they are hungry and they need to have some foods.

I found them entering in a restaurant and I went with them. One of my classmates ordered some foods directly to the waiter without looking at the menu and after we are done with our foods, I noticed that one of the group mates is asking the group leader to pay the bill. The group leader was astonished as he had not offered the meal and said that he did not have the money to pay the bill. I asked the waiter to bring the bill and we were thundered to look at the amount. It was much higher than the usual price. Though we were bit worried, but we started laughing and enjoying the whole thing. One of the classmates offered to collect all of our money and then pay the bill. We looked at our wallets, pockets & bags and collected the whole amount. There were so many changes and coins there that we had to calculate 2-3 times. But to our surprise, the total amount is still not sufficient to pay the bill.

We started laughing and I proposed to two of the group mates to give their cell phones and wrist watched as the alternatives of the bill. These two group mates got serious and were protesting that these would be an insane idea. Rest of us started enjoying their reaction as we found that they have actually taken this seriously. One of your group mates proposed that we should pay the amount we have with us and ask the manager of the hotel to allow us time to pay the rest of the amount. I told them that manager would not allow that and would call the police! We enjoyed the event, the dubious looks on some of your classmates and the fact that 2-3 of them have taken the whole thing very seriously and are actually got anxious.

We stayed there for about 1 hours and notices that people around us were giving surprising looks as we something very funny and interesting is going on among us. One of my group mates' house was nearby and he proposed that he would go home and bring the money and in the meantime, we would stay there until he arrives. We agreed and waited for him another 20 minutes or so. In the meantime, one of the boys told that the classmates who left won't come back. We laughed at the idea and acted as if it's going to happen for real. After our classmates returned from home, he paid the bill (*with some tips as well*) and then we left the restaurant.

We then left for our home and I took a taxi and paid the taxi fare from my home. I told the story to other classmates next day and they found it very funny and interesting as well. This event became famous in our class and we often mentioned the funny things happened that day among us.

Sample Cue Card 52

Talk about a new law you would implement where you live to make it a better place.

You should say:
- ➢ What law would it be
- ➢ Will it be easy to introduce such a new law
- ➢ Will it be popular

And what the benefits of such a new law would be.

Sample Answer:

The place I currently live in is a big city called (*say the name of the city or are you live in*) and it has got lots of problems and issues which need to be addressed. We have lots of laws and rules and many of them need amendment and better implementation. If I am in a position to impose a new law to make my city a better place to live in, I would make a new law that would make it mandatory for every house owner to plant at least 10 trees in their area and would prohibit cutting any tree unless permitted by the law enforcing authority.

A country should have at least 33% trees and forest of the total area for a natural balance in the country and the existing percentage of trees and forest in our country are alarmingly lower than that. Particularly in our city, this rate is almost less than 5% which makes it an imbalanced city to live in. It is not easy to enhance the forests in this city as it is a populated city and has very minimum open space. So making this rule a mandatory one would help us make the city greener and better.

Currently, most of the house owners do not have trees in their premises and there are places where this can be done. So if every landlord of the city plants some trees and takes care to grow those properly, that would improve the environment of the city. Moreover, the house owners should not be free to cut any tree whenever they want. They need to take permission and give proper reasons if they really need to cut any tree.

This would not be an easy law to implement. Lots of house-owners would not be interested in following this newly implemented law and would complain that there is no spare space for doing it. However, if the law is implemented and imposed, over time that would be achievable. Once the consciousness and necessity are understood and we start feeling our obligation towards the Mother Nature and our society, many people would feel the importance of it.

This new law would have a great number of benefits. There is no alternative than to plant trees and keep the environment healthy and this law would make our city a better place to live in.

Sample Cue Card 53

> # Talk about a gift that you gave to someone recently.
>
> **You should say:**
> - What was the gift
> - Whom did you give it to
> - How did you feel about it
>
> **And explain why you chose this gift.**

Sample Answer:

The gift I gave to my younger sister recently is the one I would like to talk about. I gave her a cell phone recently. The model of the cell phone is Sony Experia Z and it has Android Operating System. This is a water resistant cell phone manufactured by Sony Mobile and is a hot one in the market. The cells phone cost me around 40 K and I had to save the money for the last 6-7 moths to present her the gift.

I knew that she had been wishing to buy a smartphone for a year but could not do so. I thought to buy her one on her next birthday and started saving the money. I saved almost 7-8 k each month and just before 3-4 days of her birthday, I bought the phone.

I felt really great after I gave the gift to my sister. That was an unexplainable pleasure, amusement, satisfaction that I felt after I saw her bewildering face after she opened the gift. She was so happy that I felt like that was a perfect gift for her. I am sure I would not have felt the same pleasure as I felt giving her the gift doing something else. She had been longing to own a smartphone and after receiving it from me she hugged me.

As I already told, from her conversation I knew that she wished to own a smartphone that she would be able to use the internet and take quality photographs. From that day, I promised myself that I would buy her one. And I wished to buy her a really good one. I could have bought her a phone for 10k but seriously I wanted to give her the best one that I can accommodate.

> # Describe an unusual or interesting thing you did recently.
>
> **You should say:**
> - ➤ Where did you do it
> - ➤ When did you do it
> - ➤ Who did you do it with
>
> **And describe why it was unusual or interesting.**

Sample Answer:

Few months back while our visit to a friend's hometown, all of a sudden a friend proposed us to go inside a nearby forest and have a picnic there. This was a plan proposed by Arnold (*say one of your friends name*) and 4 of our friends agreed to do so.

This was bit dangerous as people scarcely go inside the forest and from the local people we have heard different scary and wild stories about this jungle. Our main attraction was the abandoned house inside the jungle and we planned to do the picnic there and take photos of wild lives and the abandoned house. We knew that my friend's guardians won't permit us to do that and hence we planned not to let them know about it upfront.

On a Thursday morning we left the friend's house and bought the necessary ingredients, vegetables, foods and other things that would be required for us to do the picnic. We entered inside the jungle and to our surprise the inside was much more open and beautiful than we thought it would be. With some difficulty we reached near the abandoned house and spent time till the afternoon. This was a very exciting and unusual experience for us. We collected some woods and made an arrangement for cooking. We eat the food we cooked and that was horrible in taste. However, we were looking for the adventure and interesting stuffs so a bad food did not kill our spirit. We could not enter the abandoned house as it was blocked and very fragile. We took several photos of the place and we notices some of the wild animals were observing us with suspicion.

I have to confess that was a bit dangerous and imprudent thing to do but we enjoyed our interesting and unusual picnic inside a forest.

Sample Cue Card 55

Describe a training session that you have attended.

You should say:
 - Where it was
 - What it was about
 - What was the most exciting and memorable part of it

And explain what you learned from the training session.

Sample Answer:

Throughout my academic years I have attended many training sessions and today I'd like to talk about the training session that I attended 3-4 years back when I was in 2nd year of my graduation. The training session was on Advanced Microsoft Office and presentation on Power Point. As a B.B.A student, I had great interest in computing and I attended the session with an enrolment fee of 500. The session was organized by a career building organization in our city and they had a good reputation of conducting successful sessions and training programs. Many of my classmates attended the session that held on the 3rd floor of the company's building.

Initially we had some doubles about what we would learn from the session as we already knew the basic Microsoft Office functionalities. But after the session started we found that the session was organized by some professionals and aimed for those who already knew some basics.

The session started at around 10:00 am and ended at 4:30 pm with 2-3 breaks. During the session, the professionals who were conducting the training, talked to us about numerous career related topics and their way of presenting those was very exciting. They told us many interesting facts and sometimes joke as well and we could not restrain ourselves from laughing. The training part went well and was interesting as well since we have learned many new things from it.

The advanced office functionality they presented was amazing. I never knew that those things were possible with the programs I already knew. Later on the power point presentation session went very well. We learned so many things and became very excited. I was so interested that I went home in the evening and at night I tried those lessons and functionality on hands with my computer.

Sample Cue Card 56

> # Describe your most favorite math teacher.
>
> **You should say:**
> - ➢ Name of the teacher and which class he taught
> - ➢ Why do you like him
> - ➢ How does he teach
>
> **And explain how he influences students to learn math.**

Sample Answer:

As my major was Science both in school and college, I had Math in every year and there are so many math teachers that I met throughout my academic year that I can't remember all of their names. Among this large number of teacher I consider Mr. / Mrs. (*say a teacher name*) to be the best math teacher who taught us math. His/her full name was (*say the full name*) and we called him/her with his/her second name which is (*say his/her second name*).

She/he taught us math in our grade 6 and his/ her way of explaining math and solutions was unmatched. She/he had been successful to make an impression that math is a very important subject and is far more interesting than some other subjects.

I like him/ her because of his/ her excellent way of teaching, his/her good behavior and honesty. He/ she always started a story before explaining any math and then she/he co-related this story with the math. She/he taught us different formula of math with a context and thus we could easily memorize those tough formulas. She/he never forced for homework and had been very patience to explain things over and over again. I'm sure the interest that grew in me on Math had been influenced by him/her.

The well-known fact that *'a good teacher delivers lectures and an excellent teacher inspires his students'*- is completely applicable for him/her and in my opinion, she/he is an excellent teacher.

Sample Cue Card 57

Describe the environmental pollution in your city.

You should say:
- What type of pollution it is
- Cause and effect of pollution
- Why it had happen

And explain how this pollution can be controlled.

Sample Answer:

I live in (*say the name of your city*) and this city has got some several issues related to environmental pollution. The major environmental pollutions that this city has are water pollution, air pollution and sound pollution.

The main reason for these pollutions is overpopulation and a rapid and unplanned industrialization of this city. The city has more than (*say the current population of this city*) whereas the number should have been far less than that. It is evitable that a large number of populations in a small city always cause environmental pollution as they use more cars, consume more energy and natural resources and create more wastages ad noises.

The reason for the water pollution is the uncontrolled number of industries, factories and other constructions that have been grown up beside the rivers. These factories and industries produce a large number of chemical and other wastages which directly affects the water. Inappropriate and uncontrolled construction is another reason for water pollution in our city. The effect of water pollution is severe, the water supply would be affected and the supply of safe and clean water would be threatened. A large number of people rely on the water available of the rivers and they would be directly affected. Lots of people would get sick due to water pollution and those diseases can become epidemics if not controlled and that results in an immense loss of innocent lives.

Air pollution is also very concerning in this city and the chemical smoke, carbon dioxide and carbon monoxide emitted from automobiles and industries are the main reason for air pollution. This city has more than million automobiles and thousands of industries which are omitting the dangerous gases, and ingredients which are causing the air pollutions. Air pollution is the direct reason people suffer from various dangerous diseases including lung cancer, asthma, heart disease etc. In fact the number of people currently suffering from these diseases in alarming and if steps are not taken to prevent air pollution immediately, this number would rapidly increase.

Sound pollution is produced by the loud horns used by the cars, loud sound used for announcement and cacophony created due to loud sound. The airplanes that fly over the resident area created a very loud noise as well. Air pollution is a silent killer that causes lots of serious diseases including hearing and brain cancer. The air pollution directly affects the natural balance by affecting the wild lives.

The most important thing to reduce pollution in our city is to create public awareness. We are mostly creating that pollution and endangering ourselves, the Earth and other species. Without our awareness and strict determination to prevent our city from pollution, we can't reduce or prevent it. Strict laws should be introduced and be applied against any environmental pollution and all the illegitimate industries and companies should be banned. The decentralization of industries and offices can be effective as it would reduce the number of people currently living in this city.

Job opportunities and other facilities should be improved in the rural areas so that people can manage works in their own cities and villages other than coming to this city. The education and morality are two important aspects that help people understand the necessity of keeping the city clean and healthy.

> ## Describe a TV program which has made a strong impression on you.
>
> **You should say:**
> - What kind of TV program it was
> - When you saw the TV program
> - What the TV program was about
>
> **And explain why this TV program made such an impression on you.**

Sample Answer 1:

I do not watch TV that often nowadays but when I was a student, I used to watch televisions a lot. There are lots of programs that really liked and watched regularly. In those days I watch mostly news and some selective TV programs. The TV program that made a strong impression on me was a documentary that I watched on Discovery Channel.

The TV program was called "*The sacrifice of genius*" and it was a serial that had around 20 episodes. I watched all of those episodes and enjoyed a lot. This was mainly a documentary serial which emphasized the sacrifice the famous and genius scientists like Marie Curie, Thomas Edison and 8 other scientists.

I watched the TV program in my third year of my graduation program. In our local time, the program was broadcasted at 8.00 pm every Wednesday. The program showed the life and work of the famous scientists and the sacrifices they made for humans and to make the world a better place. These stories were presented in a fascinating way and were very professionally made. The spectators would have the impression that they were actually watching the real scientists and their works.

I have learned so many things about those scientists and learned the sacrifices they made. Those sacrifices were unbelievable and after watching this program, I could not stop thinking about those famous scientist and their supreme sacrifices. This program has helped me thinking in a different perspective that sacrifices for others can be more important than personal achievements like wealth, fame and self-awareness. I later searched about details of those scientists and other famous persons as well and learned many things. I was actually inspired by this program and started learning closely about the people who made the world a place where we no longer need to live in the dark and do not have to fight the wild animals to earn our foods.

Sample Answer 2:

My favorite television program is an old television series which was produced during the 80's in America. The title of the film was MacGyver and it was an action TV series. MacGyver was produced for about 5 consecutive seasons, and it was considered as one of the top rated TV serials in its era.

RCTI was the local television station in Indonesia that broadcasted the program. The TV series was usually played once a week for about one hour, and I remember that it was played on Thursday Night at 8.00 pm. So as a teenager during that time, I would have sat in front of the television from 7.45 pm and waiting for the program to start. On the next day, my friends and I would discuss about what happened in it, to talk about how cool and exciting the episode was and how smart and talented the MacGyver was.

The unique thing about it is that the main character, MacGyver did not like to use gun as his weapon. Instead of using riffles, he used his creativity in creating tools to fight his enemies. I remembered that in one of the episodes, where he was locked by his enemy in a garage. But then with his creative thinking, he found some tools that could be used to open the gate of the garage, and he could escape from his enemy. I believe that we could learn some positive things from this series. We learned that we should avoid using guns, and we should also be encouraged to use our creativity. I believe that MacGyver had influenced so many teenagers during my era and I hoped that it could be remake in the future.

Sample Cue Card 59

> # Describe one of your favorite electronic media like TV / printing media / radio etc.
>
> **You should say:**
> - What is it and why it's your favorite
> - What do you do with it
> - Why it's useful for you
>
> **And describe the advantages and disadvantages of this media.**

Sample Answer:

My favorite electronic media is TV and I guess this is the most popular electronic media in the world. With the popularity of the satellite and diversity and quality of the programs offered by different channels, people started liking the TV programs more than ever. With the TV satellite network connection, watching more than 500 channels cost a very little amount.

Television offers various kinds of channels and people can easily pick the channels they like. News, Movies, documentary, entertainment, soap opera, music, sports, and lifestyle channels offers entertainment as well as different information and news. People heavily rely on TV news for latest and international news. The audio visual representation of news and information in TV are easier to grasp than other media like radio and magazines. I watch news, documentary, movies and music on TV. There are lots of channels that offer specialized programs for people and among them I find National Geographic, Discovery, BBC are very reliable and authentic source of information.

I can't always catch up with the newspaper and can easily get updates from TV in few minutes. I get sports news and can watch live games on TV. The main advantages of television are the ease with which it offers news, information and entertainment. One can easily watch TV while getting involved in other tasks which is quite impossible for other media like print media. The variation of program and channels offered are helpful for people to easily pick one's favorite channels. We can watch live events and news on TV and with the advancement of technology it has become easier for everyone to own a TV.

The main disadvantage of this media is that, it is addictive. People become addicted to TV programs and thus often spend more time watching TV than they should have. Biased news sometimes mislead people and causes non-avoidable conflicts. Too much time spent on watching television has some health issues and specifically harms kids who watch TV for a long time. Apart from that, Some TV channels broadcasts programs which are not suitable for all and this can cause harms to people.

Sample Cue Card 60

Describe your favorite subject in your academic life.

You should say:
  - ➢ What is it
  - ➢ Why did you like it
  - ➢ Your experience of this subject

And explain why you liked it.

Sample Answer:

History was my favorite subject in my academic year and I have learned so many things from the history books I read and learned from teachers related to history and they were so interesting that I later did my graduation majoring History.

Learning about the past history is something that gives us real knowledge about our country, the world and about the human race. I read History in my grade 8 and found it very interesting. This subject taught us about the past of your world, how the social and economic condition was and how the world has been shaped with the different events throughout the time. After that, I become so interested on this subject that I started reading books on History from different writers. There is a famous saying that, "*to shape the future you must know the past*" and History teaches us that. I had been lucky to have some great

148

teachers who have tremendous way of explaining the topics of History. To me, other subjects like literature and Math were also interesting but I felt a different passion on History.

After I finished my school, I took History as my major and that has greatly influenced me the way I look at the world and to the past and future. Reading and learning history was like traveling through time and generations that excited me so much.

Speaking Part 3

In this part, you will be asked furthermore questions regarding to the topic you talked in the part 2. This will give you an opportunity to discuss more ideas and issues. This part lasts between 4 and 5 minutes.

Things you should do:

- Listen for keywords in the question.
- Ask if you don't understand.
- Give details, examples and reasons appropriately.
- Stick to the topic.
- Always think you will do well.
- You can build a good vocabulary before you take the test. Always remember that practice is the key.
- You can relate the question to your own life and give answers.
- Use modals appropriately.

Things you shouldn't do:

- Don't memorize answers.
- Don't worry if you make mistakes. Go ahead. Sometimes they expect it.
- Don't go off topic.
- Don't use too many 'umms' and 'ahhs'.
- Don't use 'I think' too much.
- Don't use 'that's a good question' more than once.
- Don't worry if you have an accent.

You can be prepared for this part while you are practicing for the part 2. Just think what kind of questions can be asked in this part related to the part 2. Ask questions yourself and answer them. Practice loudly. Let your brain to familiar with the words. Let the speaking English to be a habit of you. Practice every day as much as possible. Collect more vocabulary. You can use an English dictionary to have a good vocabulary. If you are using Oxford advanced learner's dictionary or Cambridge advanced learner's dictionary, you can correct your pronunciation as well. You can either digital or the paper back dictionary. I recommend using these dictionaries.

By simply following this guide book, you can achieve a good band score like 8 very easily. Don't waste your valuable time while you plan to do IELTS. Get the maximum usage of your time. Target a high band score for every component of the IELTS test. This is a complete guide of the IELTS speaking component. Get the maximum usage of this guide.

I wish you all the best!

Manufactured by Amazon.ca
Bolton, ON